Every Day
is a Great Day!

A biography of David J. Martin, Sr.

David L. Tijerina

Scripture quotations marked NIV are taken from The Holy Bible, New
International Version®, NIV® Copyright © 1973, 1978, 1984, 2011 by
Biblica, Inc.® Used by permission. All rights reserved worldwide.

Scripture quotations marked KJV are taken from the King James Version.

Edited by Donna Martin Evenson and Lydia Cammann

Anita P. Davis, *North Carolina During the Great Depression: A Documentary
Portrait of a Decade*, McFarland and Company Inc., Jefferson, NC, 2003.

K. Todd Johnson, *Historic Wake County; The Story of Raleigh and Wake County*
HPN (Historical Publishing Network) Books, San Antonio, TX, 2009.

Thomas M. Byrd, *Around and About Cary*, Edwards
Brothers, Inc., Ann Arbor, MI, 1970.

The Echo, The Senior Class of Cary High School, 1945,14.

ISBN: 978-1-4834-9976-5 (sc)
ISBN: 978-1-4834-9977-2 (hc)
ISBN: 978-1-4834-9975-8 (e)

Lulu Publishing Services rev. date: 06/07/2019

FOREWORD

What a book! What a man! What a family! What an honor to be friends with the Martin family. David and I have been friends over 60 years! We both were in the Cary Jaycees back in the late 1950s. and I feel as though I shared a part of David's life all the way! I have always been impressed with his work ethic and his love of the Lord.

Jerry Miller

David J. Martin Sr. (left)
and his good friend and Cary Artist, Jerry Miller.

CONTENTS

PROLOGUE

A Glimpse of Things to Come

"For I know the plans I have for you," declares the LORD,
"plans to prosper you and not to harm you, plans to
give you hope and a future." (Jeremiah 29:11 NIV)

One day when David Julian Martin, Sr., was 12 years old, he delivered *The Raleigh Times* newspaper to the Esso gas station at the corner of Reedy Creek Road and East Chatham Street in his adopted hometown of Cary, NC, and something caught his eye while he was there. He noticed a few men were clearing a lot next to the gas station. It was overgrown with weeds and briers, but what piqued his interest most was not the clearing they were doing; it was the yellow and red Tru-Ade[1] sign he saw on the lot. It was nailed to a 4x4 post and an identical sign was nailed on the opposite side. David asked the men if he could have the signs. After they completed their work, the men gave them to him, and he took them home. David had lived through the Great Depression and had learned not to throw anything away. He might need them later. Besides, he figured he would make something out of them! Not long after he acquired the signs, Garland Jones, construction superintendent for the new Cary High School Stadium, gave David some used form boards that had been placed around the school's football field. Mr. Jones' construction crew had poured concrete into the form boards to build curbing around the perimeter of the running track to separate it from the football field. Ever the resourceful young man, David pulled the nails out of the wood, straightened them, and scraped the remaining concrete off the wood.

---

[1] Tru-Ade was a very popular non-carbonated soft drink sold during that period.

Then the idea hit him. He would use the signs and the wood to build a chicken house; then he would raise and sell chickens! He decided right then and there his chicken house would be built in a way that would enable him to feed the fowl efficiently. He had watched farmers build their barns as high as 8 and 10 feet tall only to put their chickens on the ground and pour their food into a pan. Those chickens would fight and claw their way to the pan to try to get their share of the food, and a lot of it ended up on the ground. David thought that was wasteful, so to keep from making the same mistake, he built a double-decker, four-foot-square chicken house. He designed it so that each chicken stall was less than two feet high.[2]

David planned to sell the chickens before their heads touched the top of their compartments. David recalled how he constructed the house: "I built that house and I put the feed on the outside, in a trough I made and attached to it. I got some orange crates to use as stalls, and I made little slats in them. They'd stick their heads through that to eat, and they didn't waste a bit of that food. Then when I got it built, I didn't have a nickel in that house, but I was ready to raise small baby chicks."

A rendering of the chicken house, drawn in 2018 by Joe Cable, graphic artist, architect, and real estate agent, as well as David's good friend and fellow church member.

David stocked his chicken house with "50 of the best sick chickens" he

---

[2] Peggy Van Scoyoc, "Transcript digitally recorded interview with David J. Martin, Sr.," 28, Sept. 2010,13-16.

could find at the Cary Hatchery, owned by the Cary Poultry Association and located at the corner of West Chatham Street and Harrison Avenue. He explained that, if any of the hatchery's chickens were weak or crippled, the employees threw them in a barrel so they could dispose of them later. David convinced the owners to allow him access to the barrel and to give him the baby chicks he wanted. Once they were in his possession, he nursed them back to health. "I'd feed them with a medicine dropper," he said. "I'd even put sulfur in the feed because Mother used to give us sulfur for a lot of different ailments. And I probably gave them enough sulfur to kill them." David ended up raising 48 of the 50 sick chickens he was given—two died—which he said was a decent mortality rate. "I just know the Lord honored my efforts," he said.[3]

With the money he made from selling his chickens, David decided to expand. He paid $8 to Mr. Bill Smith for an old construction shack, located at the intersection of East Chatham Street and Durham Road and on the same property as Mr. Smith's service station. When it was time to move the building, David borrowed a railroad jack from his friend, Dabney Craddock, an engineer on the Seaboard Railroad. Mr. Craddock lived at the corner of Kildaire Farm Road and Pleasant Street in Cary. Though he was a boy, David carried the jack with him while riding his bike a few blocks to where the structure sat. "It's amazing, you think, of a kid my size being able to carry a railroad jack," David said. "But I worked all my life, and I was a young man. I carried it with me on my bicycle over there."[4]

The building was about 8 feet wide, 8 feet high, and 16 feet long. Even though David was strong, it was too much for one person to handle, so he rented a truck for $1.50 from Carter Holleman, the local ice delivery man, a critical job in those times when most folks had iceboxes, not refrigerators. When it was time to move the building, David used the jack to raise it; then he worked quickly to remove the foundation blocks and throw them inside the building. Mr. Holleman backed his truck under it. David let it down onto the truck bed, and only an hour later they had moved the building to its resting place in Mr. Joe Smith's pasture, located across the street from where David lived. "I was in the chicken business then, sure enough. That was a miracle," David said. "A kid can't do that!"

---

[3] Peggy Van Scoyoc, "Transcript digitally recorded Interview with David J. Martin, Sr.," 28, Sept. 2010,13-16.

[4] Peggy Van Scoyoc, "Transcript digitally recorded Interview with David J. Martin, Sr.," 28, Sept. 2010,13-16.

But moving that old construction building was just the beginning for David, and afterward he added floors to the structure so he could raise more chickens. Next, he convinced the people in charge of the Durham Farmers' Exchange to let him raise all the chickens he could take on consignment. When they were old enough to sell, he took them back to their owners and made a profit on each one sold. "It's just great to be able to use your mind and think, and then use your muscle and work," David said, as he recalled the incident. "I've seen a lot of people who are always praying and never working. I believe in putting feet to your prayers and the Lord will honor and bless you. But if you don't, you're in trouble." [5]

Since that time in the early 1940s, David Martin, Sr., has become a well-known builder and developer in North Carolina's Triangle Area[6]. He is the president and owner of a variety of companies, and he has formed partnerships and a trust to benefit his children and grandchildren. Collectively, those entities do business as Martin Properties. Under the Martin Properties banner, David and his family have built, owned, and managed single-family and multi-family housing, office space and shopping centers. When David built his first chicken house, he was just trying to help his mother bring in money for their family and had no idea what the future held for him. But the ingenuity and hard work he put into building his chicken houses provided a glimpse of things to come. It is also an example of how the love and self-sacrifice he exhibited toward his family, his visionary outlook regarding work projects, his work ethic, his resourcefulness, and his faith in God enabled him to succeed in his endeavors. This book tells the story of David and his family and how the many friends he made along the way, and, above all, the Lord Almighty helped "the poorest boy in Cary" not only to survive but to succeed.

---

[5] Peggy Van Scoyoc, "Transcript digitally recorded interview with David J. Martin, Sr.," 28, Sept. 2010,16.

[6] The greater metropolitan area comprised of Raleigh, Durham, and Chapel Hill, NC.

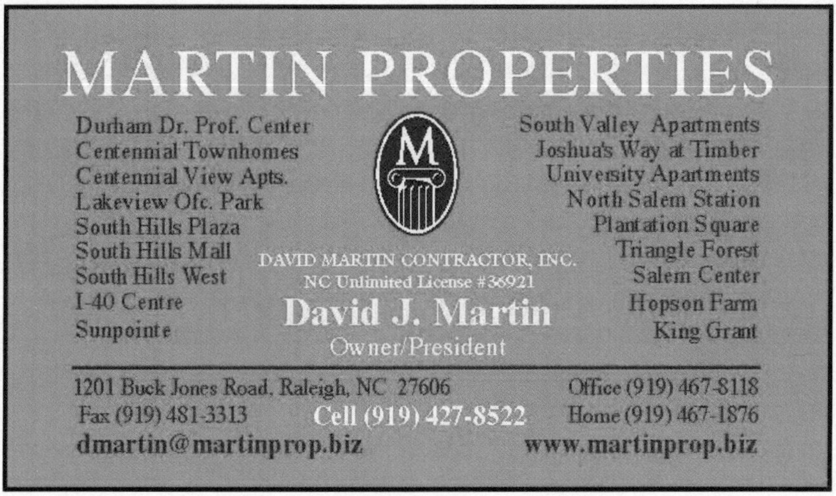

David J. Martin's business card.

CHAPTER 1

The Early Days

God is our refuge and strength, an ever-present
help in trouble. (Psalm 46:1 NIV)

David's parents, William Lafayette Martin, Sr. and Euva Perry O'Briant Martin, were married December 5, 1925. Euva was a young widow whose first husband had died during the 1918 Flu Epidemic, and she brought three children into the marriage: Mary Blanche "M.B.," Solomon, and George O'Briant. The couple's first son together, William "Billy" Martin, Jr., was born in 1926, not quite 18 months before David, and his sisters, Euva Martin Freeze and Martha Martin Grissom, were born after him. David was born a year before the Great Depression, on February 15, 1928.

David's, mother, Euva O'Briant Martin holds him
at about 1 year old at a storefront.

At the time, the Martins lived in Seagrove, NC, a town in Randolph County, close to the center of the state. When he was 2 years old, his family moved from Seagrove to the Northside area of Creedmoor, where his mother had grown up. Creedmoor, in Granville County, is in north-central North Carolina. Later, the Martin family moved from Northside and lived close to an old motel within the town limits of Creedmoor.

Even before the stock market crash in October 1929, it was a difficult time to be a parent in North Carolina.[7] Then on October 29, 1929, the stock market crashed, and the effects of this financial calamity were felt for the next decade—until 1939 at least. During this period in American history—the Great Depression—in an almost domino-like fashion stocks were devalued; banks closed their doors; people lost their life savings; industries failed; unemployment rolls skyrocketed into the millions. Teachers saw their salaries reduced by as much as 40 percent in 1934.[8] In their article "The Great Depression," Douglas Abrams and Randall Parker stated that among the hardest hit were farmers. Their 1933 gross farm income fell to 46 percent of its 1929 level. Farmers then had to deal with new crop regulations imposed on them by the federal government.[9]

While living through the Great Depression was difficult for nearly everyone, things grew even harder for Euva and her children when, before Martha was born, William Martin, Sr. became seriously ill. He later died of cardio-renal disease. This left her alone again, and with seven children to raise. "One great thing I had going for me was I had a Christian mother," David said. Facing life as a widow, Euva exhibited her strong faith in God throughout her life but especially during the many tough times her family faced. David recalled the time his family lived in Creedmoor as a "hard and tight" experience and the first time he realized he needed to do something to contribute to the family. Though he was young, he learned to split wood to help keep his mother and siblings from being cold. "I learned to be tough early on; I had to be to survive," he said.

In the winter David often wore shoes that had holes in them. With

[7] Anita P. Davis, North Carolina During the Great Depression: A Documentary Portrait of a Decade (Jefferson, NC: McFarland and Company Inc., 2003.) 8.
[8] "Great Depression," NC Pedia (published online with permission from the Encyclopedia of North Carolina) 2006, keyword: Great Depression.
[9] K. Todd Johnson, Historic Wake County; The Story of Raleigh and Wake County (San Antonio: Historical Publishing Network Books 2009) 67.

little to no money coming in, he would go barefoot in the summer, and, when winter approached, his mother would buy him a pair of tennis shoes for 50 cents.

David (left) and his brother Billy (right) wearing clothing their mother made them.

As he grew older, it bothered him that his family did not have enough money coming in to buy new clothes, and he was embarrassed when his mother went to school events wearing a threadbare coat. Also, very disheartening to him was the fact that she had to make t-shirts and underwear for him and his siblings out of old feed sacks. "Back then they didn't have shops where you could turn in clothes and give to others; there were no Goodwill Family Centers," he said.

Though things were tough for his family in Creedmoor, David does have good memories of living in the town, which was then known as the horse and mule capital of the state. He loved to watch Boots Mangum herd wild-western horses and mules off train cars and into his stables. The stables were close to the town's Baptist Church and provided a convenient location for Boots to train his horses.

David also enjoyed visits with his maternal grandparents, Tom and Lela Gooch Perry. Mr. Perry operated a country store near the small community of Stool Tree, near Creedmoor. Sadly, Mr. Perry died suddenly in May, 1933, when David was only 5 years old. David vividly remembers this event, because he happened to be in the same room with his grandfather when he died. David was visiting his grandmother, Lela Perry, who was sick in bed. His grandfather entered the room, propped a chair against the bed, sat down, and, in David's words, "fell over dead." Eighty-five years later, when David recounted the story it was still a sad memory for him and a reminder that, in his words, we all are "only a heartbeat away from eternity."

When he was about 6 years old, David's older O'Briant siblings began to leave the house to get jobs or start families of their own. Solomon married and worked on his father-in-law's farm at Northside.

George and Solomon O'Briant during their school days.

George had a variety of jobs before beginning work at the American Tobacco Factory in Durham. Mary Blanche, or "MB," as she was known to her family, was hired by the Southern Bell Telephone and Telegraph Company in Raleigh, the state capital. She rented a house near downtown Raleigh at 314 E. Martin St. It was large enough to accommodate her mother and younger siblings, and she helped them make the move. "I remember we lived close to a bakery, and I'd get cookies for a penny a piece," David said.

Moving to a new city meant attending a different school. David and

Billy attended Thompson Elementary, only two or three blocks from their house. On their first day of school they each had a two- and-a-half cent meal; at lunchtime they shared a honey bun they purchased for 5 cents. [10] The Martins may have moved, but the impact of the Great Depression could be felt in Raleigh and greater Wake County, too. In his book, *Historic Wake County*, author K. Todd Johnson wrote that, "six of Raleigh's eight banks closed between 1930 and 1933 and the closings of Caraleigh Cotton Mills, Mellrose Knitting Mills, and Wendell Hosiery Mills affected hundreds of families in the city. Other textile operations were forced to downsize their workforces, and town governments went bankrupt or resorted to bond issues to meet their obligations."[11]

Just before David began second grade the family moved again, this time to the country, just south of Raleigh and into a portion of Mrs. Lillie Hopgood's home, at 1521 Crosslink Rd.

Euva O'Briant Martin holding Martha Martin Grissom, around the time they lived with Mrs. Hopgood. Also pictured (from L to R) are Billy Martin, Euva Martin Freeze and David Martin, Sr.

"She rented most of the house to us and gave us a good deal on the

---

[10] Chris Hubbard, "Profile David Martin," The Cary News, 26, Sept. 1998: 1B.

[11] K. Todd Johnson, Historic Wake County; The Story of Raleigh and Wake County (San Antonio Historical Publishing Network Books 2009) 67.

rent," David said. Besides renting from Mrs. Hopgood, Euva, David's mother, provided care for the elderly lady. For her part, Mrs. Hopgood was glad to have the Martins in her home.

A look at Mrs. Hopgood's house as it looked in 2017.

She was a lonely widow, suffering from chronic depression and anxiety after her husband died. "Mrs. Hopgood was so depressed before we moved in she had planned to shoot herself with a 12-gauge shotgun," recalled David. Later, Mrs. Hopgood told Euva that if it had not been for her love and care she would have committed suicide. While Mrs. Hopgood did not use her shotgun on herself, it did sear a permanent memory in Billy's mind. He recalled that while at Mrs. Hopgood's house for a visit, their older brother George had offered to clean the weapon for her. Not realizing the gun was loaded, he accidentally shot a hole into the kitchen floor. When the dust cleared, Billy said Mrs. Hopgood was not angry at George; she was just glad no one was hurt!

Though they lived with Mrs. Hopgood, the Martins still faced financial difficulties. One day, before catching the bus to Garner Elementary School, David put on his ragged hand-me-down shirt that was full of holes. To keep from being embarrassed, he wore a sweater over it. When he made it to Mrs. Crane's third-grade classroom the heat was unbearable. Classrooms at the school came equipped with a radiator for use during cold weather, but the thermostat on the unit in Mrs. Crane's class was not working. She told her students that they should take off any outer layers of clothing so they could cool down. Despite the heat, David refused to take his sweater off.

The fact that they were poor did not keep David and his brother, Billy, from having fun or finding things to do. One day while they lived with Mrs. Hopgood, David paid a boy $1 for a bike that was missing a back tire. He took a water hose, ran wire through it, fashioned it into a tire and put it on the bike. Then he painted the bike red and—presto—he had transportation! "At night, I'd stand by and admire it because I got something to work out of nothing," David said.

Through all the changes that occurred in the Martin family's life during that time, one thing that remained constant was their mother's faith in God. The family would walk a little over three miles one-way in every type of weather imaginable to attend services at Tabernacle Baptist Church, facing Moore Square in downtown Raleigh.

CHAPTER 2

A Place to Call Home

Religion that God our Father accepts as pure and faultless is this: to look after orphans and widows in their distress and to keep oneself from being polluted by the world. (James 1:27 NIV)

The Martin family's prospects began to improve shortly afterward when "M.B." went shopping for furniture for her own apartment, which was just down the road from where her mother and younger siblings lived. She ended up making her purchases from Cooper Furniture Company in downtown Raleigh. She was talking with her friend, W.E. or "Earl" Cooper, the store's founder, and learned that there was a house available for rent in the nearby town of Cary. The house was at the corner of Kildaire Farm Road and Pleasant St. and had three bedrooms. It was a great fit for a mother and her four children. It rented for $12 a month. "We had running water, David said. "You'd grab a bucket and run out to the well to get it. We had a running toilet too. You'd have to run out to the privy house out in the backyard to use the bathroom, you might say."[12]

When the Martins moved to Cary, the town had a population just above 900, roads were still unpaved, and the city government suffered due to lower property valuations and a shrinking tax base. Times were rough financially for most of the town's citizens too. When the Bank of Cary closed its doors in June 1931 its losses and liabilities totaled $53,000. Deposits lost totaled $22,000, including many customers' life savings.

---

[12] Peggy Van Scoyoc, "Transcript of digitally recorded interview with David J. Martin, Sr.," 28, Sept. 2010, 5.

Even after the federal government stepped in to shore up the nation's banks, it would be a long time before some Cary citizens deposited money in a bank again. As for the closure of The Bank of Cary, in his book, *Around and About Cary*, Thomas M. Byrd relates that the bank's failure during the Depression and the town's financial woes were no surprise to state banking officials. They knew that Town Attorney and President of The Bank of Cary, James M. Templeton, Jr., had abused his position. Not only had he reneged on the terms of a loan the Board of Commissioners had made to him, but he also had mishandled $30,000 of Town funds from the sale of bonds for its water works. The Town was forced to sue him.[13]

The misappropriation of funds by a formerly respected community member and the stock market crash did not dampen the generosity of the people of Cary. They extended helping hands to the Martins in a variety of ways. "Mother would say—when we were down to nothing to eat for that night—'The Lord will provide. The Lord will look after his own,'" David said. "I'd think she was crazy because we needed something to eat. But you know the good people of Cary. Somebody would show up and bring us something. It was just a wonderful experience to know that people cared and would help you." [14]

Lovie Mathews, pictured in 1996, gave clothes to David
and his siblings when they were in need.

---

[13] Thomas M. Byrd, <u>Around and About Cary</u>, (Ann Arbor, Edwards Brothers, Inc., 1970) 87.

[14] Peggy Van Scoyoc, "Local developer recalls his childhood," <u>The Cary News</u> 20, March 2013: 7A.

One example of this occurred on a day when David was riding his bike on Academy Street, and Wiley Jones, who had been sweeping his walkway, motioned for David to stop, went into his house, and came out with a box of saltine crackers for David to take home. Lovie Matthews, whose husband worked for the highway department, would catch a train to Raleigh and buy clothing for the Martins. "She gave me a striped shirt and some other clothes," David recalled.

Dabney Craddock, the most prosperous man in Cary at the time, came to the aid of the Martin family when he sent them a 20-pound bag of flour at a time when they were badly in need. "Had it not been for that flour, we would have had nothing to eat in the house," David said. "The Craddocks taught me how to give." Still others were generous to his family, too. David recounted the following story: "One day when I was at Denning's Grocery store, I started to buy some groceries but I lost my dollar. I looked all over that store, but I couldn't find it. There was a Primitive Baptist preacher operating the store, and after I got home, he drove up to the house and told me he had found my dollar. Now I don't think he found my dollar. He found that dollar in his pocket, but he drove all the way to our house to give it to me. People were just good to us. We did all we could, but you don't refuse when someone offers you something out of a heart of love."

The Martins did not just take handouts. Though David was just eight years old, he rode around on his bike and did whatever odd jobs he could to bring in money for his mother and siblings. One such job was helping to tend other people's gardens and chicken houses.

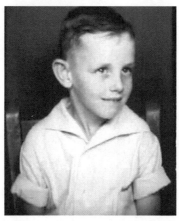

As a boy of 8, David rode his bicycle around in search of odd jobs.

One of his early customers was Mary Warren Yarborough, the wife of the Cary Mayor, Dr. Frank Yarborough. "Everybody, including doctors had gardens back then," David said. He explained that people in the town also shared gardens that were at the end of a row of houses. "I'd tend the garden, but one thing they had me doing that I didn't like was— Mrs. Yarborough would have me plant those beautiful flowers around her house. I thought that was foolish because you couldn't eat them. Everything was dedicated to survival, and it was tough. But it was a great learning experience."

When David was 10 years old, he picked blackberries and sold them throughout Cary for five cents a quart. Anything not sold the family would can and keep for later use. "We'd end up with 200 quarts of blackberries sometimes," he said. "If you eat 200 quarts of blackberries from one season to the next, you'd about turn into blackberries. When we got married my wife, Marilyn, brought home a can of store-bought blackberries, and I said. 'Honey, if you don't ever bring another blackberry here it will be too soon.'" [15]

David also sold Lancaster seeds and the weekly *Grit* newspaper, published in Williamsport, Pennsylvania. Self-described as "America's Greatest Family Newspaper," the *Grit* was quite popular among rural communities at the time. When he was old enough, David was hired as an independent contractor to deliver *The Raleigh Times* newspaper for $2.53 a week. "I had 21 customers in Cary when I took it over, and in nothing flat, I tripled it," David said. "I got up to 63 customers." Prospective customers were gracious and responded well to a young man who each day traversed an eight-mile rural newspaper route on a bicycle, all in an effort to help his family. "I brought in over half the money in our house when I was 11 years old," David said. "The rest was welfare."

Though most people in Cary saw how hard David worked to bring in money for his family, not everyone treated him well. He faced a considerable amount of stigma due to his family's financial status. This was evident when one day at the age of 10 or 12 he went into a grocery store in Cary to purchase a candy bar for his mother—a rare treat in those days—using change left over from food stamps he had spent. David shared this about the incident: "I was checking out and I got a candy bar,"

---

[15] Peggy Van Scoyoc, "Transcript of digitally recorded interview with David J. Martin, Sr.," 28, Sept. 2010, 6-7.

he said. "It was a nickel-candy bar and it was the most candy I could get for a nickel. The lady checking it out said loudly, 'Boy, don't you know that you can't get candy with food stamps,' and everybody in the store could hear it. To me, that was so embarrassing." That incident helped to fan the flame of his desire to help his family end their dependence on welfare and gave him the motivation to do whatever was needed to accomplish that goal.

At one point, despite suffering from a carbuncle that caused pain to shoot up his leg every time he moved, David hired himself out to a farmer, Mr. Bob Sauls, to cut and shock—or stack—his corn. Pain or no pain, he remained focused and gritted his way through cutting and shocking 16 acres of the crop. When he finished, he was rewarded for his perseverance with half the profit from the sale of the corn. Later, he attached five bushel baskets to his bike and began selling apples around town that he bought for $1 a bushel. He sold them for 50 cents a peck—effectively doubling his money. He showed that natural gift for making a profit again when he rented Bob Saul's mule for 25 cents an hour and charged people in Cary 50 cents an hour to plow their gardens. "When I was making as much as a mule made, I thought I was somebody," he said. He also tended and cleaned people's chicken houses. One summer, he took a job working for Miss Nanny Leach, a retired school teacher who lived across Academy Street from the Yarboroughs. She had about a dozen chicken houses and she hired David to help her build floors in them. "She'd have dirt and sand hauled in and take them and put them in layers to create the floors," David said. "That's the way they used to build roads too."

Once the building materials were brought in, Miss Leach and David would spread a layer of clay and a layer of sand on the ground and pack it real hard. This is how David described his first week working for Miss. Leach: "I started working for her for 10 cents an hour, and she would try to get me to put down the shovel and rest. I thought when you hire out to someone, you work every moment. I didn't know you had breaks. I'd be perspiring and she would want me to stop and rest, but I kept working. So, the first payday, she paid me twelve and a half cents an hour instead of 10 cents. I got a 2 and a half cent raise, and I've learned, if you apply yourself, people will hire you."[16]

[16] Peggy Van Scoyoc, "Transcript of digitally recorded interview with David J. Martin, Sr.," 28, Sept. 2010,12-13.

David was not picky about the jobs he took. He would take any odd job, no matter how unglamorous it might be. For a little while, he made money digging toilet pits at $5.00 a hole. Working or beating the bushes for other ways to earn money did not leave time for anything else. For instance, David could not make the jump from Cub Scout to Boy Scout because he was too busy working. "When the other kids were out playing, I was working," he said. One person he did make time for was his younger sister, Martha. He made sure that she and his sister Euva had what they needed. She remembers him as being a "caring and protective brother" who did a lot of things with her. "We picked blackberries together, and when he found a penny or a nickel he bought me candy."

CHAPTER 3

A Great Friend

One who has unreliable friends soon comes to ruin, but there is a friend who sticks closer than a brother. (Proverbs 18:24 NIV)

When David's family moved to Cary, his mother enrolled him in the third grade at Cary Elementary School. His teacher there was Miss Eula Williams, and it was in her class that he met one of his best friends and future brother-in-law, Joseph "Joe" Samuel Grissom. Joe said he believed he and David became friends because they had similar quiet demeanors, and they came from poor families. But the major difference between him and David was that Joe's father, Joseph Stephen Grissom, was available to provide financially for his family but David's was not. In fact, when the two were in school, it wouldn't be a far stretch to say that David went to class in between his jobs. As one might expect, juggling school and work affected his grades. Joe recalled: "In grammar school, I made better grades than David did, I believe. When I went home after school, all I had to do was pick up a little firewood and study, and I did. I put a lot of time on books. I made better grades in high school than David did, but he had other places to put his time and other interests, such as providing for his family."

In fact, since Joe rode a bus to and from school he had no idea that David was working during that time. Most of the students who rode the bus to school thought people who lived in town were rich, he said. He would not come to understand the depth of the Martin family's dependence on David until the two boys were young men in their 20's. But though Joe may not have caught on to the fact that David had to carry the load as a father would have done, there is no doubt the two were friends. On the rare occasion when he was not working, David's favorite pastime was riding his bike. One day he and his older brother Billy rode their bikes out to where Joe lived. Joe shared this brief story: "I lived like four or five miles from Cary then, and I lived in the sticks—no electricity, no telephone. They found out where I lived. I came out one afternoon, and there was Billy and David in my yard. David said, 'I just wanted to see where you live—to see you a minute.' Then David and Billy went on their way."

While it is true Joe did not have to work like David during his grammar school days, things were not much easier for the Grissom family financially. Prior to the Depression, Mr. Grissom worked at the Old Company Mill and as a custodian at Camp Craggy, where the local Boy Scout troops camped. As times grew harder, just prior to the United States entering the war, he took a job with the Works Progress Administration (WPA) gathering metal in preparation for the looming conflict. The WPA was the major program President Franklin Delano Roosevelt used to help some of the millions of unemployed people in the U.S. get back to work. But even when the man of the house had a job, some families still had to rely on the government for assistance. Joe's family was one of them: "I remember when the days of welfare came along, Daddy would go to Raleigh to see the welfare office—we called it welfare then, not social services—and he'd get food supplies for the whole neighborhood. He'd come and distribute it to people that were hungry, that needed things, and us too. I remember that went on for quite a few years. Everybody was poor," he said. "We were poor as old Job's turkey. You know, the turkey was so poor and sickly he had to lean against the house to gobble." Things might have been difficult for the Grissom family, but Joe noted they always had something to eat, whether they ate beans, prunes, or fat back all week. "For a treat on a Saturday night, coming back from town, my Daddy would bring a block of ice, and we'd have frozen ice cream to eat," he said.

Not all of David's and Joe's friends or classmates were subject to the poverty caused by the Depression. Like the rest of the state and country, some people's family businesses did not go under; they actually prospered. The family of their classmate, Doris King Carroll, fit into that category. They owned King's Peach Orchard, a 70-acre-farm filled with peach trees located on Lake Wheeler Road where the NC State turf farm is today. "Money grew on trees for me," Mrs. Carroll recalled. In fact, her family continued to do well after the Depression and during World War II. However, her family, like the Martins and the Grissoms had to adjust to food, clothing, and gas rationing imposed by the federal government during the worldwide conflict.

Yet, while David and most of his peers faced tough circumstances during World War II, he was learning lessons in Julia Rand Woodard's sixth-grade class that began to open his eyes to the possibility that his life could change for the better. This realization first occurred when Mrs. Woodard broke up a clique of boys who had taken control of a football given to them by their home room mothers. These boys would not let anyone outside of their group have the ball. Their selfishness was significant because the person who had the football automatically became the captain of a team and was given the right to pick his team first. David recalled how Mrs. Woodward addressed the situation: "She said, 'I believe in democracy, don't you?'" Then she developed a weekly system that no longer gave any importance to who controlled the football and instead rotated the captaincies to two different boys in the class. Those boys, in turn, were given the opportunity to build their teams as they saw fit. "And one week, the poorest boy in Cary had the privilege of being the captain of a team," David said. "She gave me some thoughts that maybe I could make it in life; I wouldn't have to stay on the bottom rung all my life."[17]

David also enjoyed the method Mrs. Woodward used to teach history lessons. She brought a little radio to the classroom, sat it on her desk and turned it on so the students could hear President Roosevelt's speeches. "'And this is the way she would talk," David related. "She said, 'Listen, listen! This is history being made—right now!' And she made her teaching come alive. She developed people into useful citizens, and so she was my favorite teacher all the way through grammar school, high school, and even when I went to Carolina.'"[18]

Mrs. Woodard was not the only one who inspired David. A famous statesman of the day helped him learn to persevere too. "One thing you need to know about me is that I never give up," David explained. "I

---

[17] Peggy Van Scoyoc, "Transcript of digitally recorded interview with David J. Martin, Sr.," 28, Sept. 2010, 7-8.

[18] Peggy Van Scoyoc, "Transcript of digitally recorded interview with David J. Martin, Sr.," 28, Sept. 2010, 7-8.

remember listening to my radio in Cary, early in World War II, and I heard Winston Churchill give his famous speech to Parliament where he said the British would fight on the beaches, in the fields, and in the streets and that they would never, never, never surrender. It was quite a moving speech. I heard it as a young man of 12 years old, and it stirred me."

"One thing you need to know about me is that I never give up. I remember listening to my radio in Cary, early in World War II, and I heard Winston Churchill give his famous speech to Parliament where he said the British would fight on the beaches, in the fields, and in the streets and that they would never, never, never surrender."

–David J. Martin, Sr.

The effect of the lesson David learned from Mr. Churchill was evident later that year, when he was hired to take a mule to a blacksmith shop near the old Cary Hatchery to be shod. The mule started acting up, and while David tried to get it to move along the dirt road that later became Kildaire Farm Road, it "put on brakes" and threw David over its head! "Then the mule backed up, and if he'd come forward, he would have trampled me to death while he was looking at me," David explained. But David didn't give up, because if he had told his boss he could not get the mule to the shop, he would have been fired. Instead, David got back up, summoned all of his intestinal fortitude, and started over. Eventually, man and beast made it to the blacksmith shop at the corner of Harrison Avenue and Chatham Street. David held the mule by its hind foot while nails were hammered into its shoe. But that ornery mule was not finished with David yet! While he was holding its foot, the mule started to wiggle and move, and before a nail was completely driven in, David was forced to let go of him. "A 12-year-old boy just couldn't hold that mule," he said. "When I had to turn him loose, that nail ripped me open on my hand. You know, even that was a good experience. You never give up because you have adversity. I never give up."

Soon afterward, David went into the chicken business for himself and built his famous chicken house out of two Tru-Ade signs. Not surprisingly—especially with a mother who taught Sunday school in every church she attended—that same year, at the age of 12, David also made a commitment to the Lord and was baptized at First Baptist Church in Cary.

CHAPTER 4

High School Days

Whatever you do, work at it with all your heart, as working for the Lord, not for human masters. (Colossians 3:23 NIV)

Cary did not have middle schools back when David was a student, so he began his high school days as an eighth grader in the fall of 1941.

His class was the last one to graduate from Cary High School as eleventh graders. In North Carolina up until that time, there had been no twelfth grade. When his class began their freshman year, there were 91 male students and 70 female students.[19]

The winds of war and the aspirations of the leaders of Japan, Germany, and Italy for world domination would play a major part in winnowing the number of male graduates in the class of 1945 down to about 10, with David being among them. Though World War II began in 1939, the U.S. did not enter the conflict until December 8, 1941, the day after Japan's infamous surprise attack on Pearl Harbor. In 1942, Congress lowered the draft age to 18, but, if their parents

David wearing the striped shirt Mrs. Mathews gave him his freshman year.

---

[19] The Echo: The Senior Class of Cary High School. Cary: Cary High School 1945, 14. Sherry Williamson, "Community Faces Hard Times," Cary High School Centennial Celebration, Special Edition of The Cary News, 5, June 1996: 33.

gave their permission, boys as young as 16 could enlist in the Armed Forces. Some of the young men who dropped out of Cary High School to join the war effort met the age requirements. Others simply lied about their ages. Still another group of young men dropped out to take good-paying defense service jobs and rationalized their guilt over leaving school with the sentiment that, after all, they were helping in the war effort. [20]Among them would be David's brother, Billy, who went to work for a company that was the forerunner of today's hi-tech enterprises. Later in the war, he served his country in the U.S. Navy. David stayed in school and continued to take care of his family and bring in money however he could.

Whether during the school year or in the summer, David could be found working. When he was 13 years old, he worked at a chicken farm, 12 hours a day, six days a week for a $6.00 paycheck. One male teacher and role model who helped him quite a bit during his time at Cary High School was R.S. "Dad" Dunham, the vocational agriculture teacher. He helped transport the loads of David's chickens to the farmers' market in Raleigh so they could be sold at wholesale prices. Mr. Dunham also took his students to his own 16-acre tract of land, later the site of Glenaire Retirement Community in Cary, and taught them how to cut timber and plant trees. "He was teaching us that you could take a piece of land and make something out of it," David said. He also credited "Dad" Dunham with helping to teach him and his classmates how to have a good work ethic and, on a very practical note, how to drive. In their beloved teacher, David and his classmates also saw a man who gave to his community by, for example, arranging for the town's old cannery to be used to help can food for servicemen during the war. "He had a heart for people that needed help," David said. "He had a cut-down, flat-bed, Ford Roadster truck we nicknamed the "doodle-bug," and he taught us how to drive on it. He was quite an asset to the community."

While David gained insight about how to make land work for a person from "Dad" Dunham, his own hectic schedule did much to create his strong work ethic. David not only raised chickens for the Raleigh Farmers' Market during high school, but he also owned two cows whose milk he sold for 10 cents a quart on his way to school. Since his family

---

[20] Sherry Williamson, "Community Faces Hard Times: Cary High School Centennial Celebration," Special Edition of <u>The Cary News</u>, 5, June 1996: 29.

did not own pasture land, every day he would take the cows with him and stake them out along the edge of the school property to graze. During his lunch period, he would run home with the cows, water them, and then run back to school to stake them out again. Having completed that task, he would run to the downtown area of Cary to hitchhike a ride to his job at the Piggly Wiggly Grocery in Raleigh. David explained that the reason he could keep up this schedule was because he arranged to take his last two classes as study periods. Instead of studying, however, he skipped them and went to work. "I didn't have time to study," he said. "I didn't even carry a book home but once or twice the year I was a senior. Then I didn't have time to study it. In other words, it was from noon to way after dark that I had something to do."

David's work before school had affected his reputation and Joe said as the two advanced to higher grades in school, he became known for being late to class. "He would always come in late and the teacher would sigh and make a remark something like, 'OK, what is it this morning?' And David would say, 'Oh the chickens were getting out; I had to fix the fence; or I had to stake the cow out before I left;' or some reason that he just didn't have enough time."

*Joe Grissom was a member
of David's graduation class in 1945.*

David shared the following story about how it could sometimes be difficult caring for his cow: "I remember one morning when the cow dashed out. I didn't lock the gate and I was milking the cow and the cow was housed in a garage there, just a little one car garage you might say. But the cow was in there, and the feed room and chickens and I'd milk the cow. That morning, the cow got away. I chased her all over the hillside. Every time I was taking a breath, it was just like a knife cutting through my lungs. I was so out of breath. I got that cow home and I took a strap, a leather strap, and I was beating that cow." [21]

David and the family cow, Daisy, in 1945.

"My mother came out there and got all over me about doing that. To think that she had raised a son that would mistreat a cow. She got so excited that she had a heart attack. I promised the Lord that I would never whip that cow again if he would let my mother live—and she lived to be 88 years old!"[22]

Mishaps with animals he cared for and time constraints he encountered might have given him a reputation of being late during his high school days, but any negativity was more than compensated for by David's increasing self-confidence, which was fostered by encouragement from his teachers, along with his innate charisma and natural friendliness. He took debate and dramatics classes, and was the basketball manager for the school. He also showed his school spirit when, during his junior and senior years, he stepped up to fill the gap on the Cary High School football team left by the shortage of male students. Joe and David, inseparable as always, were the left and right guards on the team. David was not the biggest man on the squad, but he was certainly the fastest! He would knock down his opponent and then go downfield on a running play, blocking for the ball carrier.

Another trait that David exhibited as he progressed in school and

[21] Peggy Van Scoyoc "Transcript digitally recorded interview with David J. Martin, Sr.," 28 Sept. 2010,10.
[22] Peggy Van Scoyoc, "Transcript digitally recorded interview with David J. Martin, Sr.," 28 Sept. 2010,10.

which rose to a crescendo during his high school years, was a thirst for useful information. "David was never satisfied with just sitting in class—even in the lower grades—unless he could really see that something was pouring into him—he was getting something out of it," Joe said. "He would get restless and would want to go and explore and want to find something else, to see what other avenues were available. David was always busy seeing about the activities of everybody and everything that was going on, because he had to have an idea of what was going on."

Perhaps the greatest example of how far David had come from the quiet third-grader at Cary Elementary School was how he spearheaded his school yearbook staff's effort to revive *The Echo*, the Cary High School annual, his senior year. The high school had not had a yearbook for about 15 years due to the lean times the town had endured during the Depression and the war. David decided two months before his class graduated that they should have one. However, he ran into some resistance when Mary A. Underwood, the economics teacher at the school and a past yearbook adviser, went to Thad N. Frye, the principal, and told him the students did not have enough time to produce an annual. David convinced Mr. Frye it was possible, and the students set to work on the project. "Mr. Frye wanted to help me any way he could," David said. "We did it without an advisor and the staff—we did it ourselves." David exhibited his perseverance, relatability, and selling skills when he and fellow senior Wilbur Jones went to Raleigh to sell some ads for the annual. Their first day out they came up empty-handed. Wilbur gave up, so David went out alone the next day and for many days afterward, but he met his goal! A similar thing happened when some of the female staff members were unsuccessful persuading area businessmen to buy ads. David took over, approached the same men again, and successfully sold the ads! In the end, *The Echo* was published before his class graduated. Because David's ad campaign had gone so well, each graduate received a free yearbook. *The Echo* named David "Class Rambler," and also described him as "Slow but Sure" and "Ad Hunter."[23]

Though he seldom took a book home or did much homework, David had learned there were usually four topics in a paragraph and in his history class, for example, he would read the assignment just before the teacher called on him and answer her question correctly. However, he did not remember the information as well as he would if had he studied the night before. Somehow

---

[23] The Echo: The Senior Class of Cary High School. Cary: Cary High School1945, 7.

his teachers took pity on him, probably because they knew about his situation. They did not penalize him for failing to turn in his homework. [24]

David was the first male in his family to graduate from high school.

He may have graduated "by the skin of his teeth"—but he graduated! David's mother was proud that he was the first boy in his family to graduate from high school, and even more proud that he had done so while holding multiple jobs.

---

[24] Peggy Van Scoyoc, "Transcript digitally recorded interview with David J. Martin, Sr.," September 28, 2010, 9.

CHAPTER 5

Venturing Out

*Anyone who does not provide for their relatives, and
especially for their own household, has denied the faith
and is worse than an unbeliever. (I Timothy 5:8 NIV)*

The year David graduated from high school, 1945, also marked the end of
World War II. On September 2nd, U.S. Army General Douglas MacArthur
accepted Japan's surrender aboard the USS Missouri in Tokyo Bay.[25]
After David graduated, he worked for Advance Auto Parts for a short
time before enlisting in the U.S. Coast Guard on March 7, 1946. Even
though Germany and Japan had both surrendered the previous year, the
world was still in turmoil. The U.S. Veterans Administration considers
anyone who enlisted in the Armed Forces before the end of 1946 a WWII
veteran. That includes David.

His friend, Joe Grissom took a different path and joined the Marines
around the same time. David attributed the reason he became a Coastie,
as coast guardsmen were called then, to his admiration for the uniform
his friend and fellow Coastie Doug Holleman wore on visits home after
he entered the Coast Guard. "He had that fancy suit that looked like he
was an Army colonel," David said. "It was sporty looking, though I never
got past wearing that bad-looking seaman's dress-blue uniform."

David went to boot camp on the East Coast. He apparently took the
physical conditioning in stride, but perhaps had some difficulty with

---

[25] The National Museum of American History The Japanese surrender on board
the U.S.S. Missouri in Tokyo Bay on September 2, 1945. http://americanhistory.
si.edu/collections/search/object/nmah_1303405

hair grooming regulations! After his third week of training, he sent a photo of himself to his mother. In the photo, he was wearing his dress uniform, and underneath his hat, he sported a shaved head. On the back of the picture he wrote, "<u>RESTRICTED:</u> Don't show this to anyone 'ever' under any circumstances—still no hair."

David during U.S. Coast Guard boot camp.

After graduation from boot camp, he was posted at the Coast Guard Motor Machinist School in Groton, CT, where he received his advanced training. When he completed the course, he was promoted to the rank of third-class petty officer (E-4), jumping the rank of 2nd class seaman (E-3). David achieved the higher rank because of the skills he acquired during the class which included: how to work with diesel engines, gasoline, heating and air conditioning, fluid flow, plumbing, welding, and anything else he needed to know regarding how to maintain the inside and outside of his assigned ship. He explained that since the Coast Guard has fewer personnel than the Navy, motor machinists are taught many trades, a practice which helped David obtain and renew an unlimited contractor's license for over 50 years.

David later served in the Coast Guard's seventh district aboard the USCG Sweetgum, and the USCG Samuel Travis—both of which were cutters, vessels designed for speed rather than size. He was based at Curtis Bay Station in Baltimore, Maryland. The ships on which he served patrolled the entire East Coast of the United States, from Portland, Maine down to Key West, Florida. In some cases, their duties even took them to the northern shores of Cuba! Besides protecting American waters against foreign intruders, the crews often performed heroic water rescues in less than ideal conditions. David recalled. "When other people were running from the storm, we had to go into the storm! We were all over the place!"

David might have left home, but he never let up on his commitment to support his family in Cary. He sent over half his monthly paycheck home to his mother and sister, keeping only $6 a month.

David on leave from the Coast Guard with his mother, Euva O'Briant Martin (left) and sister Martha Martin Grissom (right).

His entrepreneurial spirit still intact, he augmented his remaining funds by purchasing an iron and charging willing Coasties to wash and iron their clothes. Later, he expanded and started making money cutting hair, too, so he could go on liberty. "I always went on liberty," David said. "I always went to town."

One thing he enjoyed doing while in the Coast Guard was boxing. One of his commanders was Jack Dempsey, the World heavyweight boxing champion, from 1919-1926. Commander Dempsey was known to have shared some of his sparring techniques with the men under his command. David also had the good fortune of learning to box from Mike Perry, Joe Louis's sparring partner. Mr. Louis was another great heavy-weight champion who won 66 fights—49 by knockout. Mr. Perry did not just teach David how to box; he taught him how to knock people out. David was awarded the title of middleweight-boxing champion of Curtis Bay Station.

After serving two years, two days, and two hours David's enlistment with the Coast Guard ended. He chose not to reenlist and headed home to Cary. He had received great instruction and training and had enjoyed being away from home, but his working environment was made increasingly difficult by a mechanical officer with poor leadership skills. This situation soured his daily life in the Coast Guard. "The man in charge of the engineering room was hateful—a rascal," he said. I probably would have stayed in 20 years, if I would've had a good commander." Never one to spend everything he earned, when David left the Coast Guard, he had a significant sum of money in his savings account.

David is grateful for the chance he had to serve his country in the military. He deeply appreciates the training he received and the life lessons he learned while serving. To this day, he remains a strong supporter of his fellow veterans as well as all men and women on active duty. He is a lifetime member of the American Legion.

CHAPTER 6

Home Again

*Repent, then, and turn to God, so that your
sins may be wiped out, that times of refreshing
may come from the Lord. (Acts 3:19 NIV)*

When David returned home to Cary in 1948, his mother and sister Martha were living in the Cary High School teacherage,[26] where his mother was the cook. He moved into the basement there.

A page of the ledger Euva Martin used at the teacherage.

---

[26] Several of the Cary High School instructors lived in this building, adjacent to the campus.

Though he was a highly skilled Coast Guard veteran, David was unable to find work as a machinist in the area. Before long the habits and work ethic he had developed as a boy kicked in again, and he set about making money any legal way he could. He worked virtually around the clock-except for the brief periods he slept each night.

David said he was "always doing more than one thing" then, and indeed he was. He was very active as a grading contractor in the Morrisville-Green Level, NC, area. His work included excavation, land-clearing, and digging farm ponds. In addition, David paid $1,200 for a dilapidated house on East Chatham Street and worked every free night he had remodeling it. Later, he rented a building on the 500 block of E. Chatham Street and operated a Shell gas station there during the day. He chose a strategic location, near what later became a roundabout formed by the intersection of Chatham Street and Durham Road. The same building was later occupied by the Jackson Hewitt Tax Service. The station was a bit of a wild place then. Younger people hung out there, smoked, and told "nasty jokes." Often, the smoke was so thick it was hard to make out who was there. David recalled: "And I was right in the midst of them—smoking, cussing, and telling raunchy jokes with the best of them." Unforeseen by David at the time, an old friend would later intervene and change this state of affairs.

In the meantime, while he might have had a little time to socialize at the gas station during the day, David did not have time for much of a nightlife. Instead, he began making a name for himself as an independent contractor delivering dry cleaning for Jim's Cleaners, owned by Jim Bland. While he worked for Mr. Bland, David was determined to knock on every door he came across between Cary and Chatham County—a little over 24 miles away—to offer his services to potential customers. When David made deliveries, he worked well into the night. "I could knock on anybody's door and get a percentage of the dry-cleaning fee from the customer," David said. "I earned 25 cents on every $1 of clothing I delivered. I was very thorough. I'd stop by every week, whether they had anything to turn in or not. I kept everybody clean." Crayton Lynn Banks, a classmate of David's brother Billy, was impressed with the speed at which David made his deliveries. "I mean he would not walk—he would run when he made a delivery," Mr. Banks recalled. David's classmate, Floyd McConnell, said he agreed to let David deliver his dry cleaning on the condition that his suit be ready for church on Sunday mornings. "My wife would say, 'Alright. Go see if you can find a suit for this morning,' and it would be there," McConnell said. "It's funny to think, sometime during the night, he left that suit." Other people in Cary were also good to David when he delivered their clothing. Mrs. Bettie Moore King set a plate at her table for David if he came by around lunch or dinner. David, knowing how generous she was, would often arrange his delivery times so he could take her up on her hospitality. He was acquainted with the Kings because Mrs. King's husband, Walter, was the produce manager at the Piggly Wiggly Grocery where David had worked while in high school. David's sister Martha was also in the same class as their son, George. When David started delivering dry cleaning, Jim's Cleaners had about eight competitors. Because of David's persistent advertising and follow up with customers, that number dwindled to only one before he stopped delivering clothing for Mr. Bland.

Sometime between running the Shell gas station during the day, delivering clothing in the afternoon, and remodeling the house on East Chatham Street overnight, he found time to attend college for about four semesters with his good friend Joe Grissom. Joe completed his enlistment with the Marines about the same time David completed his Coast Guard service and moved back home too. The two took advantage of their GI Bill benefits and enrolled at the University of North Carolina at Chapel Hill (UNC). At the time, David's dream was to go on to attend law school after graduation from college. He had a burning desire to become a lawyer who would represent "the underdog." He carpooled with Joe and sometimes with W.T. Cooper. W.T was a WWII veteran and the son of Earl Cooper, the same man who had suggested David's family move to Cary and had provided them with food when times were particularly tight. Eventually, David's plate became so filled with responsibilities that he had to withdraw from school. Joe recalled their conversation when David told him he would have to leave school: "I said, 'Why? What are you quitting for?' David said, 'Well, I have to find a place for Mother and my sister to live. They're tearing down the old teacherage, and they have to have somewhere to live. I've got a couple of ideas, and I have to work on it. I just don't have time to work on it and to go to school too.'"

The conversation drove the idea home to Joe that David was not the average carefree young man in his 20's. He was responsible for the well-being of his family. As for David, he said his intention was to take a semester off and then re-enroll at UNC, but due to his business pursuits, he never returned. Before long the ambitions of Communist leaders on the Korean Peninsula would force Joe to leave school for a time also.

After David found a place for his mother and sister to live—a house in front of the one he was remodeling on East Chatham Street—he made a decision that helped him get closer to God and put an end to the smoking, swearing and raucous behavior at the Shell station. It all came about after a visit to a dry-cleaning customer who also happened to be his friend W.T.'s grandfather, Mr. Billy Cooper, who owned and operated a farm on Trinity Road. David described the incident in a letter he wrote to his friend W.T. in 2015, congratulating him on his ninetieth birthday:

> "Your Grandfather, Mr. Billy Cooper, invited me to a revival at Ephesus Baptist Church. The speaker, Dr. Charles Howard, was a "ball of fire" evangelist! When he was finished, David Martin did not just go up to shake his hand. I got down on my knees and got right with the Lord! And I haven't had to cuss anybody out since!"

David was so inspired by his renewed commitment to God that he started inviting everyone he encountered to church and encouraging them to accept Jesus Christ as their Savior. One of the first people he invited to the Sunday services was Joe Grissom. However, Joe did not feel the need to go to church at that time. He recalled: "I wasn't going anywhere. I said, 'Oh, OK.' (I don't know if I had any wheels then or not. I don't guess I did.) David said, 'I'll come get you.' The next week, and I said, 'I don't know if I want to go or not.' David said, 'I'm going to come knock on your door.' I said, 'NO, no, no, no.' He did come and knock on my door. I lived in the front part of a big old house, and he knocked on the window. I'd be inside the bedroom and I'd get up. I told myself, 'Doggone it. If he's going to come here every Sunday morning and wake me up like this, I'll get ready.' David did that a number of times before he started me going to church a little bit. He was persistent."

David's forthright way of trying to persuade Joe to enter into a personal relationship with Jesus Christ would not be the last time he tried to persuade someone to turn their life over to God. As the years passed he did whatever he could to spread the word of God. "As he goes about he shares the gospel," Joe said. "He would take time from anything and go share with somebody about the good news of Jesus... that's just David. He really has the gift of evangelism." Not long after these encounters with Joe, David decided to close the Shell gas station down and also to stop making deliveries for Jim's Cleaners in order to take on a new venture.

CHAPTER 7

Up and Coming Businessman

Those who work their land will have abundant food, but those who chase fantasies have no sense. (Proverbs 12:11 NIV)

David sold the house he was remodeling on Chatham Street for $7,000, making a tidy profit. In 1951, when he was 23 years old, he purchased equipment, rented space, and opened the first of his three Martin's Cleaners locations in Raleigh at 201 E. Hargett Street.

Martin's Cleaner's location at 201 E. Hargett Street in Raleigh.

By that time, he had learned the business from Jim Bland and had a loyal customer base. "I learned just from watching people," David said. "If I saw someone do something, I knew I could do it too." Later, he opened his second store at 1216 South Saunders Street, and a third location at

711 N. Person Street. He opened a fourth location on East Chatham Street in Cary, where his employees did repair and sewing work on clothing and other items.

The Martin's Cleaners bread truck
David used to deliver dry cleaning.

He delivered dry cleaning in a former bread truck painted purple and bearing the name "Martin's Cleaner's" in gold lettering. During this time, David's different business locations doubled as his home. He would often spend the night at one of his stores after he finished making deliveries.

The year 1951 was also significant for another reason. It was the year Joe Grissom became David's brother-in-law, marrying David's youngest sister, Martha, during a hastily planned ceremony before a justice of the peace. Joe was one of the 1.5 million men who were drafted into the armed services after Communist North Korea invaded South Korea in June, 1950, with the goal of forcing their communist ideology on the entire peninsula. He was considered a "retread," the name given to people who served in both World War II and the Korean War. He loyally served and donned a Marine uniform again.

Both Joe and Martha credited David with setting up the two of them. For David's part, it was most likely an accident. The pairing occurred because David asked Joe if he would go on a double date with him. When Joe wasn't sure who he could ask, David said he would find Joe a date. David then suggested that Joe ask Martha out! The date was rocky from the start as Joe kept teasing Martha, calling her "Baby Sister," due both to her relationship with David and after a popular cartoon character of the day. When Joe called her "Baby Sister" one too many times, Martha grabbed a paper bag containing Octagon soap that David kept in his car for the purpose of sealing leaks in his gas tank. She then "whacked" Joe in the face with it! The bad news is Joe suffered a split lip, but the good news is that he never called Martha "Baby Sister" again! Furthermore, he started seeing her not just as David's little sister but as a very intelligent, attractive young lady! This new-found respect quickly blossomed into love and then life-long commitment.

Around this time David's optimism and sense of Christian morality convinced him he could make a positive impact in the lives of people around him. In April 1953, he was one of 15 people who ran for a seat on the Raleigh City Council.

Two More Candidates Announce In Race For Raleigh's Council

David J. Martin, of 709 N. Person St., cleaning establishment operator, paid his filing fee to the Wake Board of Elections Friday morning as a candidate for a seat on the City Council.

Martin's filing sent to 12 the number of candidates for City Council who have announced their intentions by paying their filing fees. Saturday is the last day for registration and filing.

One other, Willie Duke, talent scout for the New York Giants baseball club and prominent sports promoter, indicated he would be a candidate in the April 25 primary, however, he did not pay his filing fee Friday morning. His announcement was made Thursday afternoon.

A native of Randolph County, Martin has lived in Wake since 1936. He was graduated from Cary High School and attended the University of North Carolina. He also served in the Coast Guard for two years.

Martin said his principal interest in entering the campaign was largely one of doing something to raise the community's level of morals. Specifically, Martin said he would like to see the Council appoint a committee charged with responsibility of studying influences which "tend to throw the younger generation off the right track." In this connection he mentioned obscene literature now available on newsstands, TV beer commercials, and suggestive movies. Martin also advocates better pay for policemen.

Duke, 42, a resident of 314 W. Jones St., is a veteran of World War II, having entered service as an apprentice seaman, and being discharged with the rank of senior lieutenant. He served in both the Atlantic and Pacific war zones.

Commenting on his candidacy,

DAVID J. MARTIN

Duke said, "I see in the City Council an opportunity for the fulfillment of a desire to serve the City. I consider it a privilege and an honor to be a candidate. . . . To those of you who will consider me as a candidate, I'd like to ask for your vote and support with the assurance from me that I will give to the office of Councilman the time and thought required of the position."

Duke said the decision to be a candidate was his own, "and I will seriously consider all proposals with an open mind," he said.

Saturday will mark the last day for candidates to file with the Wake Board of Elections. The registration books will also be closed to voters Saturday after sunset. The books will not be opened again until after the May election.

The announcement of David's candidacy for Raleigh City Council.

The day he announced he was running for office, he released a statement advocating the establishment of a commission appointed by the city council to review how the Raleigh Police Department was structured and to study the influences which tended to lower moral standards among the younger generation. The statement read in part:

> "Some influences which I have noticed in Raleigh are: obscene literature (over half of the 250,000,000 pocket editions of literature sold last year were obscene to the point of arousing impure or lustful sexual thoughts and desires within the reader); beer advertising on TV, (we are instilling this within mere infants and where will it leave the child?), lewd movies (net similar results as obscene literature, only more impressive and upholds an industry that is certainly not making decent impressions on the rest of the world through foreign film distribution)." He added: "Morals and police protection work hand-in-hand and that is why I advocate a better police force."[27]

The election was held May 5, 1953, and *The Raleigh Times* reported that only a fifth of registered voters in Raleigh came out to vote. Five incumbents were re-elected to the city council and two newcomers were elected. Unfortunately for David, though he received 3,908 votes, he placed eleventh and did not win a seat on the council. He said it was probably for the best because it allowed him more time for other priorities.

While David resumed his normal activities after his losing election campaign, the Korean War was raging and the whole world was on edge. As mentioned previously, the United States had become involved in that war, which was the first open Cold-War Era conflict pitting the U.S. and its United Nations allies against China, the Soviet Union, and their communist surrogates, whose goal was the world-wide triumph of their way of life.

Adding to the uncertainty of the world situation, racial tensions in the

---

[27] "Final Filing Hour is 6 p.m." Raleigh Times 15 Apr. 1953:1.

early 1950s were increasing, not only in North Carolina, but throughout the United States. After the 1954 *Brown vs. Board of Education*, U.S. Supreme Court decision, conflict ensued between those who supported the desegregation of public schools and the awarding of full civil rights to African-Americans and those who did not. While other people kept their distance from areas of Raleigh with a high population of African-Americans, David was not afraid to be around people of color. He even made a point to drive through those areas with a high population of African-Americans while delivering dry cleaning. One of David's regular customers was Roxy Brewer, who lived in the predominantly African-American community of Asbury in Raleigh.

"I was pro-black before the law said black people had the right to do certain things. I felt like black people were as good as I was," he said. "In other words, I really had sympathy for them because I had been discriminated against myself because of my poverty. When you grow up in Cary, nobody as poor as you are, it makes you sympathize with people that have struggles like you have struggled."

Though many things were changing abroad and at home, things quieted down a bit for the Martins after Joe Grissom returned home from the Korean War. For a while, he took over one of David's routes and worked at Martin's Cleaners while completing his studies at UNC. Joe eventually graduated with a Bachelor of Arts degree in Political Science. He recounted the following story about an incident that occurred while he was picking up clothing from a customer's home: "My route started six or seven miles this side of Chapel Hill, came all through Carpenter, Green Level, out in the country—big route, and I'd go up to people to offer our services. A man said, 'I'm giving you this suit, and I need it back for Sunday for church.' I said, 'It'll be here, no later than 6 o'clock on Saturday afternoon.' And he said, 'You won't be on my steps at 12 o'clock at night, will you?' I said, 'I don't go to anyone's steps at 12 o'clock at night. He told me, 'The man who had this route before you did. I never got my clothes back before 12 at night.' Of course, he was talking about David, who scared people out of their wits sometimes when he made late deliveries. For instance, on one occasion just before midnight, he scared Mrs. Margaret Ellis Russell when he made a noise while delivering dry cleaning to her home on Kent Road, near Western Blvd. Her husband, Charles Russell, Jr., was a graveyard shift supervisor at the Raleigh Post Office. Having grown up in the country around guns and rifles, she kept a .357 Magnum handgun to protect herself and her twin boys, Ken and Phil, against intruders. Ken recalled that when his mother heard David, she grabbed her gun, made her way to the door, jerked it open, and aimed the gun at him, just before realizing who he was. Fortunately, she did not shoot, but David certainly got a good scare!

CHAPTER 8

Tying the Knot

*A wife of noble character who can find? She is worth
far more than rubies. (Proverbs 31:10 NIV)*

The best thing that happened to David while he was in the dry-cleaning
business was the opportunity to clean and deliver clothing for Mr. and
Mrs. Alf Broadwell. The couple lived in Green Level, what was then a
small, close-knit rural community between Apex and Cary, NC. The
Broadwells had eight children, including a daughter named Marilyn who
was five years younger than David. Unknown to Marilyn at the time, David
found out she was on the Green Hope High School girls' basketball team.

*David went to Marilyn's games
before he ever asked her on a date.*

He started going to her games before they ever dated. "He said he was coming to look at my legs," she said, chuckling. Eventually, David asked her out, but she refused to go out with him. Marilyn became more open to the idea when her mother intervened on David's behalf. "My mother said, 'Well Marilyn, I think you should date him because he seems to be a very nice young man.' So, that's how it got started."

Marilyn accepted David's invitation to go to his church, but she thought he was too forward. She did not have very long to dwell on his demeanor because on the way to the church his car ran out of gas on Western Boulevard! Marilyn recalled the incident: "He started thumbing, and I was sitting in that car, waiting for him to get somebody to get us some gas. That was our first date." Fortunately for David, Marilyn continued to date him. With little to do in the area, most of the time their dates consisted of him taking her to church, the two of them going to an occasional movie, or her helping him to make deliveries on his dry-cleaning routes. Sometimes they delivered clothing late into the night. Marilyn added that since David loves to drink milk that his delivery truck always smelled like sour milk because after he finished drinking a carton of milk he would throw the empty milk cartons on the floor!

While David's love life was headed in the right direction, time and Divine Providence would place him at the right place at the right time in his business life. In 1953, not long after he started dating Marilyn, David and Joe Grissom were driving along Trinity Road, near the NC State College Research Farm, when Joe asked David to stop so they could visit Joe's friend Charlie Hicks. David noticed Mr. Hicks had what looked like an apartment building sitting on his property. He was apparently remodeling it. After Joe introduced them, David asked Charlie what he was doing. Charlie replied that he was building a house for his wife using one of the old Vetville buildings from State College—later NC State University. Vetville and its hastily built housing units had been filled with returning WWII and Korean War veterans and their families who—like David and Joe—had taken advantage of their GI Bill benefits and enrolled at the college. Vetville was slated to be demolished to make way for the construction of Bragaw Residence Hall, a single-male student dormitory. A new married student housing complex, E.S. King Village, located on the other side of the campus, eventually took Vetville's place.

Mr. Hicks, as an employee of the college, had been given one of the buildings on the condition that he haul it away.[28]

Joe noticed David perked up when he heard where Mr. Hicks got the building and when he learned there were more available. "I wondered what in the world David was talking about and why he was so interested in that pile of junk," Joe said. "I was looking at that building, and it was about to fall down, you know. Well David, I found out later—after he left me—he went over to State College to find out about those buildings."

The buildings were at the entrance to the college, on the corner of Dan Allen Drive and Western Boulevard. David learned the college officials planned to auction them off. The day of the auction, he tendered a sealed bid on one of the buildings and purchased it for $300. Before he could move it, however, he faced a formidable obstacle. The route he needed to follow was a two-lane road crossing a highway. He approached the highway department and was given permission to move the building overnight on two conditions—that he pay for the police to block off the roads and that he move the building after midnight. David cut that building in two and moved half of it, along with the partition wall separating it from the rest of the building, to 217 Waldo St. in Cary, where he was building a duplex. Having been cut in two, the remaining half was exposed to the elements, but that did not stop David. He decided to move into the remaining portion, comprised of the living room and kitchen of the original unit. Despite not having running water, sewer, or electricity, he worked on that unit day and night. Eventually, he had to move the building. Working with only the light of a fire he started with scrap wood, David jacked up the unit so he could back a truck under it. For a second, he thought he saw it move. The flickering light from the fire made it difficult for him to judge whether the building was moving or not, but he decided to stand still. Yes, it was moving! David jumped out of the way just before it could fall on top of him. "I had to get out of the way and let it fall," David recalled. "And one end was up in one corner. It was all twisted up and the two ends were wide open. It was a mess. You know the old saying, 'When you get a lemon, start a lemonade stand,'" he said. "Well, when you have a problem, look for the opportunity."[29]

---

[28] NCSU Librarians. "Vetville Housing. "Vetville, NCSU

[29] Peggy Van Scoyoc, "Digitally Recorded Interview with David J. Martin, Sr.," 28 Sep. 2010, 23.

David knew from having seen their newspaper advertisement that the college officials planned to auction off the remaining buildings. He decided to leave his building right where it fell. He figured when potential bidders came to look at the other buildings and saw the condition his was in, they would not want any of them. These instincts proved right. "They'd walk around that mess that I had, and they'd walk off shaking their head," David said. "Not one soul bid on those buildings. It was just an opportunity, and too many people, when they have something bad happen—'oh, that's the end of the line.' I look for the opportunity." In the end, he bid on and purchased all the buildings for $300 each. Joe Grissom said many of the people who had looked at the buildings thought David had wasted his money since they were in such poor condition. They laughed at the thought of him trying to move them. But David and his men moved every one of them to Avent Ferry Road and started work on an apartment complex called Martin Homes, later to become University Apartments.[30]

While David's determination enabled him and his employees to move those buildings, he would not have gotten very far if not for Mildred King Craig. She was the sister of Martha's classmate George King and the daughter of David's onetime boss at the Piggly Wiggly. Mrs. King also happened to be the credit manager at the Montgomery Ward store in Raleigh. David was having difficulty getting a line of credit at the time, and did not understand its value. Already familiar with his strong work ethic, Mildred offered to extend credit to David's business. From that point on, he developed a great friendship with Mildred and her husband, Harold Craig, a plumber. Due to his expertise as a plumber and in gratitude for the credit line, David called on Harold to help him with plumbing jobs for many years.

When he wasn't working at Martin's Cleaners or his apartments, David was active at the Christian Missionary Alliance Church in Raleigh, where he taught the young boys' evening Sunday School class. Some might say he was a little too active in that church! He was dating a young lady who played the organ for a daily devotional radio show and who also served at the church on occasion as a guest organist. There was just one problem; David was dating Marilyn too! The young boys in the Sunday school class he taught did not like his 'other girlfriend' very much because they thought she was too aloof and self-centered. Marilyn, on the other

---

[30] Peggy Van Scoyoc, "Digitally Recorded Interview with David J. Martin, Sr.," 28 Sept. 2010, 23.

hand, often visited the class when she came to church with him. She also had endeared herself to the boys when, during the Christmas holidays, she accompanied David and the children as they went Christmas caroling through area neighborhoods. After they finished performing at each house, a child from the group offered the family a Christmas tree in exchange for a tip. The money collected went toward the purchase of a used bus which the congregation repainted and made roadworthy.

David said he started dating the other young lady because Marilyn had moved to Durham. It was too difficult for him to see Marilyn at night and then to get up to run his dry-cleaning business at five or six o'clock the next morning. But he did continue to invite her to visit his church. Things came to a head one evening when Marilyn decided to take him up on his invitation and to surprise him by attending a service. That evening the "other girlfriend' was invited to play the church's new organ—which had been recently donated by Raleigh businessman Seby Jones—who later became the mayor of Raleigh. David recalled that he sat at the front of the sanctuary, since the organist was his guest that evening. Unknown to him, Marilyn had slipped in and sat on the back row. "I surprised him alright," she chuckled. Marilyn recalled what happened when the boys in David's class saw her come through the door that evening: "Some of his boys, the ones that were in the class, went up to him and said, 'David! David! Marilyn is here!'" The rest said, "David, your other girlfriend is here!" Then they added, 'She said she wasn't going to love you anymore.'" David, in his words, tried to "hush them up."

Marilyn had parked her car right by the front door of the church. David's car, a Studebaker convertible, was parked around the corner beside the church. After the evening service the boys from his Sunday school class gathered around Marilyn's car and clamored for her attention. When David came out the front door, they rushed up to him repeating, "She said she wasn't going to love you anymore." David again did his best to "hush" the boys. Then he put the other young lady in his car and went back around to the front of the church to calm his students and explain things to Marilyn.

When David explained to the other "girlfriend" what was going on, she was indifferent to the situation, observing that she and David were, after all, not engaged. Marilyn said she never saw the 'other girlfriend' that evening and added that she was not mad at David or his date. In a humble and loving tone, she told David, "I just want you to be happy." After this incident, David knew the time would come when, in his words, "I married that girl!"

For her part, Marilyn said she was satisfied that in David she had found a solid Christian man. She recalled the emotional reaction her father had the day David asked for her hand in marriage. "David said, 'Mr. Broadwell, I need to ask you a question,' and my Dad already knew what he was going to ask and said, 'No you don't either!' He took off and went out of the room...But I was my Daddy's girl, see." Mr. Broadwell eventually gave his blessing to the marriage, after David and her mother reassured him everything would be okay. When David told his mother that Marilyn had accepted his marriage proposal, she also gave the young couple her blessing telling him, "You had better be good to her, because she's a jewel." Marilyn, who was there when he told her, chimed in with, "Yeah, I'm a jewel alright!" Marilyn and Euva Martin had a very close relationship. In Marilyn's eyes, her mother-in-law was "as good a Christian woman as I've ever seen." She added, "When we started dating, David told me he helped look after his mother and he told me, 'I'm always going to look after my mother, and if your mother needs help, I'll help her too.'"

Having been given a nod of approval from their parents, David and Marilyn began planning their wedding and were married on June 26, 1954, at the Green Level Baptist Church with the Rev. M.W. Stallings officiating. In addition to her father walking her down the aisle, her brother and six sisters were members of the wedding party, as was David's younger sister Martha and one of Marilyn's friends.

David and Marilyn were married in June of 1954.

David's brother Billy was his best man. After the wedding, the two spent their honeymoon in the North Carolina mountains. When they came home, they continued to worship and serve at the Christian Missionary Alliance Church, working with the children there.

Marriage did not stop David from working hard. When he and Marilyn returned from their honeymoon, he turned his attention back to Martin's Cleaners and the future University Apartments. He faced some challenges, however. David related this story about his experiences: Before the former Vetville buildings could be made habitable and become income producing, he had to figure out a way to run water and sewer lines onto the property. David explained how he accomplished it: "Well I got a break when a man told me he used to live on that property and there was a natural spring down at the base of a big tree that was surrounded by shrubs. I did some looking back in there and sure enough, there was nice spring of water." David said he could see water pouring out from the spring's tributary but that the shrubs—which were prickly privet bushes—covered the area and blocked access to the spring. He plowed through the area, knocked the bushes down, and discovered the spring came out of solid rock. Once he saw where the spring lay, he cut through the rock and created a small reservoir there. After he created the reservoir, David bought a used pump for $10, purchased two 5-cent washers, and had a working water pump for $10.10. "So, I put that in. Then I dug a trench and put this pipe I already had on hand in to serve those houses," he said. On his way home, he realized he needed a way to store water for the apartments. He approached officials from the Town of Zebulon, who were selling a used railroad tank car that had the capacity to store 6,000 gallons of water. He was able to purchase it from the Town for a nominal amount because the Town had built an elevated storage tank and no longer needed the tank car. That tank supplied water to the apartments for many years until city water and sewer service became available.

Once the water lines and water storage issues for the apartments were addressed, David's next task was to put in working sewer lines. He requested and was granted permission to haul away cinders from a nearby state-run school that used coal-fired boilers. He loaded them by hand into an old pick-up truck and took them to the apartment site. "Then I put in septic lines, using the cinders from my leach-bed filtering system. I got some cinder blocks and built my septic tanks."

David recalled, "I don't mind telling you, I built up some muscles in the whole process."

At that point, he felt he had built sturdy apartments and had extended adequate water and sewer lines to them. However, the Raleigh building inspector visited his work site and condemned those apartments. He told David that since he had taken the Vetville buildings apart and put them back together again, they did not comply with the city's building code. "Well, that started a whole new round of fighting," David said. "I went to the Planning Commission and argued and argued, and they kept rescheduling meetings and putting me off. They tried to put the issue into a committee several times, but I fought hard to keep that from happening because I knew a committee would never settle the issue. That was just a way to get it out of their hair."

The impasse went on for several months until near the end of the year when one of the Planning Commission members helped David out. He recalled, "He said, 'Boys get some Christmas Spirit and help this old boy out.' So, they altered the law to allow the inspector to give me some relief, and I went back to work. I put in heat and electrical wiring. Every time the inspector came by, if something was wrong, he'd show me how to fix it." Finally, David began renting apartments in 1958 for $70 a month, mostly to students and employees who were associated with NC State College. He also continued to add additional units to the complex along Avent Ferry Road, Chappell Drive, Ryan Court, and Broadwell Drive each year until 1961.

One of the apartments David moved from State College to expand University Apartments. David turned it into a triplex at 2603, 2605, and 2607 Broadwell Drive.

David said the attitude he had when he first thought about building University Apartments as well as when he approached the Planning Commission was a can-do won't quit attitude. "I didn't know how I was going to get water, sewer, and electricity put in out there, but I didn't let that stop me," David said. "I knew I could find a way somehow. When the inspector and the board tried to shut me down, I didn't just roll over and let them have their way. I fought and I fought hard. Don't get me wrong. I didn't curse or make threats or try to bribe anybody to get my way. I'm a Christian and I realize people are more important than business. I was respectful and polite when I argued with them, but I was also stubborn. They came to realize that they weren't going to get rid of me until they gave me what I wanted." Drawing on his Christian faith, he said his interaction with the commission was like the story of the persistent widow who approached the unjust judge in the Bible, as recounted in Luke: 18:1-8. He explained: "The judge did not care about her problems, but he knew she wouldn't quit until he helped her out. So, you see, being persistent and not giving up is Biblical. Doesn't God tell us to knock and to seek? And I have been told that the scripture means that you don't just ask, knock, and seek one time. It means that you should keep asking, keep seeking, and keep knocking, until you have your answer. Sometimes you have to fight. You can't get discouraged just because you face a few obstacles, especially if you are a Christian. If you are called of God and are doing His work, then you should succeed in what you put your hand to. The Bible says, 'If God is for us, who can be against us?' That is a principle I have lived by and have seen work over and over again in my enterprises."

CHAPTER 9

Fatherhood

*Train a child in the way he should go, and when he is
old he will not turn from it. (Proverbs 22:6 NIV)*

Along with the joy of marriage, came new monthly expenses. David
quickly realized that though he put in a lot of hours at Martin's Cleaners,
he wasn't bringing in enough money to adequately support his mother
as well as his new wife and household. "One night, we sat at the dinner
table, and all we could do was laugh because we only had 10 cents
between us," Marilyn recalled. At that time a loaf of bread cost 20 cents!
But though things might have been tight for David and Marilyn, they
made it a point not to let his mother know how dire their situation was.
Marilyn elaborated: "His mother would have had a fit if she had known
that she was eating well and we were
eating loaf bread and gravy."

The birth of their first child,
David Julian Martin, Jr., in December
1955, gave the couple another reason
to ensure they had an adequate
amount of cash flow, but those were
happy and exciting times for David,
27 and Marilyn, 22.

She recalled that the day David
Jr. was born, she told her husband
she felt sick to her stomach. David
wanted to take her to the hospital,

*David, Sr., strengthening his
infant son David, Jr.'s arm muscles.*

but Marilyn told him she thought something she had eaten was what had upset her stomach. He in turn called his mother and filled her in on Marilyn's condition. Euva Martin told him that Marilyn was not sick to her stomach, but she was about to give birth to their baby. He needed to take her to the hospital immediately! They arrived at the hospital in time for the delivery, and Dr. William Bland, the nephew of Jim Bland, David's former employer, delivered their son. Ultrasounds were not used in the United States until the 1970s, so there was no way to determine ahead of time whether Marilyn would give birth to a boy or a girl. David felt sure, however, that they would have a son. He told their family and friends long before Marilyn went into labor what he believed would happen. When Dr. Bland emerged from the delivery room, David asked him if the baby was a boy, and—perhaps to tease the anxious new father—the doctor told him he forgot to check! David did not wait around for an answer; he ran off to tell his relatives and friends that Marilyn had in fact given birth to a boy. Dr. Bland went on to deliver all six of the Martin children.

David started early instilling a positive work ethic in his young son. David Jr. at the young age of 3, was already accompanying his father to job sites and could often be spotted up on a roof with his Dad! He grew to be a quiet boy, at least in part because with five female siblings it was difficult for him to get a word in edge-wise! His father noticed that he increasingly showed a talent for working with his hands.

When David Jr. was born David and Marilyn lived in a small house in Raleigh at 1411 Simpkins Street, since renamed Collegeview Avenue. This house was actually comprised of half of the first building David had moved from State College's Vetville, the half that had fallen off the truck!

The first house the Martins lived in was one he built in 1954 at 1411 Simpkins St., now renamed Collegeview Avenue.

David had turned this structure into a tidy home at minimal cost. Lacking a refrigerator or stove, they used a hot plate to boil water and to cook their meals. To keep their food cool, they used an ice box at the back of the house. It did not work very well so David went to an auction and paid $27 for an old-fashioned refrigerator that sat on four legs. "We came up the hard way," he said.

A short time later, David decided it was time to close Martin's Cleaner's and find another job. He decided to try his hand at selling cars. When he inquired about a job as a car salesman at Harmon Motor Company, the local Lincoln-Mercury dealer, the manager told him there were no openings. However, he was welcome to fill out an application. If there was an opening, the manager promised to give him a call. When David came across the section of the application that asked what salary he expected, he filled in the space with a large "NONE," and wrote in parentheses, "I prefer a commission." When the manager asked David why he filled out the application in this manner, David replied, "This way I can set my own salary." He was hired on the spot.

David worked hard and within his first month on the job became the dealership's leading salesman. However, the man who was supplanted by David as lead salesman began mistreating him. "I took every opportunity to sell a car. He didn't want to work at night," David said. "That man had been there eight years and had a lot of repeat business. I didn't know as much as he did. I didn't know the product like he did. I didn't know how to sell cars like he did. But if I heard somebody say, 'I've got to work tonight and they didn't want to work,' I'd say, 'I'll work in your place.' Now I'd just work longer, harder hours. If you work and apply yourself in America, you can get ahead. So, I've been blessed with a good work ethic." David continued to work hard and did not allow pressure from a disgruntled coworker to upset him until the man sold a car to a customer with whom David had already been working for three weeks. When David asked the other salesmen whether their coworker had stolen other salesmen's customers before, he learned he had indeed and, furthermore, was not penalized for it. David told his manager he could not work under those conditions, and he left the company. Afterward, he applied to work at a Buick dealership and was hired. "The man at the Buick dealership wanted me to go to auctions so I could see the value of cars." While at an auction one day, David bought three cars for himself and wrote a check for them, despite not having the money in the bank to cover the purchase. Not one to back down from a challenge, he put his talents as a salesman to work, and he sold those cars before the check cleared!

*David's Auto Supermarket was the largest used
car lot in Raleigh when it opened.*

Because David actually was not too fond of the Buick brand, he quit working for the dealership not long after that episode and opened his own car lot. He named it the Auto Supermarket. It was located near where East Chatham Street becomes Hillsborough Street, just inside the Raleigh City limits, and became the largest used car lot in the city.

David moved his young family to a 32-foot mobile home that doubled as the car lot's office. He had it moved near where he kept his vehicles, after discovering that one of his employees was selling his merchandise and pocketing the money. In fact, he and Marilyn were sitting in the grandstand at the North Carolina State Fair race track watching a "Hell Riders" stunt show when David realized that one of the cars being demolished before their eyes had been stolen from his car lot. Needless to say, he fired the employee responsible and kept a careful eye on his merchandise after that!

Living on the site of their business was an interesting time for a young mother. Marilyn remembered being afraid for David Jr. when a rat found its way into their trailer. Occasionally, she had to juggle her time between tending to her son and showing cars to customers while David was away at car auctions. The upside to living on the car lot was that she had her choice of cars to choose from when she wanted to go to the grocery store. The almost comical downside was that after Marilyn finished her shopping and was ready to load her groceries into her car, she would sometimes forget which vehicle she had driven!

David eventually moved the family to the house he had been remodeling at 217 Waldo Street near downtown Cary. While they lived there the couple's daughters Donna and Dotty Jo were born in January 1957 and March 1959, respectively.

Donna

Dotty

Mrs. Martin said that after she gave birth to their first child, she did not need anyone to tell her when she was going to have a baby because she knew what to expect. She added that all six of their children were born at the "old" Rex Hospital at the corner of Wade Avenue and St. Mary's street in Raleigh. The building eventually became the headquarters of the North Carolina Employment Security Commission.

Hospital rules were different then, and men were not allowed to be in the delivery room when their children were born. Marilyn said, "I feel like he got cheated; now everyone goes in the room with their wives." The rules were different for women, too. Instead of staying in their mothers' rooms after they were born, the newborns were immediately taken to the nursery.

As their children grew, David gave a couple of them nicknames. He affectionately called Donna his Number One Daughter, but only because she was the first daughter to be born. "All my life, I thought that meant I was his favorite, but it didn't," she said. David's desire to treat all his children equally would become apparent years later when he gave each of the siblings the gift of a lot of their choice in a subdivision he developed. However, Donna said she thought she did spend more time with her father than some of her younger siblings. This circumstance could easily be attributed to the increased number of projects he was managing.

Donna was secure in the knowledge that her parents would never divorce, because they had made that very clear to the family. Like all married couples, however, they had their points of disagreement. Donna said she could hear the frustration in her mother's voice, when time after time, David showed up late for dinner or did not come at all. David's youngest daughter Debbie, who is ten years younger than Donna, added: "There was many a cold meal waiting for him because love always hopes. She would really believe that he was going to come home on time, and it was always some different excuse. But she always held out hope, and she has been an amazing wife." Donna added that because of her father's tardiness at dinner one of her biggest pet peeves to this day is someone being late.

"But he would be home when people spent the night," Donna said. "My cousins would spend the night and Daddy always told us ghost stories." But the one he told that scared them the most did not involve any ghosts. He told them how he played a joke on the owner of a boarding house, where a woman he dated was staying. The landlady held the young ladies who lived there to a strict curfew, much to David's annoyance. He told his children that he stuffed a pair of ladies stockings with cloth, put shoes on them, and stuck them under the couch so all you could see were what appeared to be two legs. When the landlady went to investigate, David pulled a leg out from under the couch, and she began screaming that it came from that "dead" body. "As Dad would tell that story, he would reach down and pull that stuffed leg out from under our couch!" recalled Donna.

Early on, David taught Donna—and all his children—the art of frugality. When she was 9 years old, he told her she had saved enough money to put in a savings account. But she was not too keen on the idea at first. Her parents had to persuade her it was a safe thing to do. "They had to convince me the bank would not be robbed," she said. Finally, she gave in, and her father opened the account for her at the Fidelity Bank in downtown Cary. David later marveled at Donna's quick-thinking when he hitched her and David Jr, to a plow, using them as "mules" to till their family garden. It seemed to be hard work for the children. David Jr. grunted as they worked, but Donna appeared to quietly pull. Several days later, after they finished, David told them he was proud of how hard they had worked. Donna grinned and said she had only acted like she was pulling the plow; her brother had done all the work! David did not discipline her, but he did keep the matter in mind.

Donna related that with her dad gone so much, her mother doled out the discipline—usually with a switch. "I only got one spanking from him in my life," Donna said. It occurred when she was 13 years old. She had become friends with a girl who was sassy to her parents. When her dad told her he needed the phone, she was sassy to him. "The phone was very important to him. He's the first person I knew to have a car phone. You know, those big square phones people used to have."

For her part, one of Dotty's earliest memories of her father involved the time he took the children on a Putt-Putt Golf outing. Her younger sister, Martha Dale Martin, called "Dale" by her family, fell into one of the small waterways on the miniature golf course, and was quickly fished out by her father. Dotty also remembered that her mother and Aunt Dot—Marilyn's sister Dot Mulholland—would take the family on vacations to Myrtle Beach. David declined to go on week-long trips with the family, due to his schedule and habit of managing many projects simultaneously. However, he would occasionally take a bus or fly in for a day or two to meet them. Marilyn was supportive of his work pursuits but always happy when he could make time for the family.

In the late 1950s, while still operating his car lot, David saw 62 acres of land on Old Apex Road in Cary that was about to go on the auction block. The land was considered to be "out in the country" at a greater distance from grocery stores and other subdivisions than most real estate professionals would have recommended at the time. Nevertheless, David envisioned building a subdivision there and foresaw the growth of businesses nearby that would support it. The day of the auction he placed a $12,500 bid for the land but had only $2,000 to put toward the purchase. When he approached a bank for a $10,000 loan and told the loan officers his plans for the land, they turned him down. When that door closed, he decided to enlist the help of Cary Powell, a prominent farmer who lived in Fuquay-Varina. David persuaded Mr. Powell to purchase the land on the condition that David could buy it back in one year but that Mr. Powell would get to keep the 1.55-acre tobacco allotment that came with the farm. Then David went to work on an advertising plan.

He advertised the sale of lots at the site, which he planned to call the Triangle Forest subdivision, by placing an ad in *The Raleigh Times* Saturday edition. The ad listed the time and date for a land auction. The day of the auction, he provided a map that showed a street, Marilyn Circle,[31] and 17 lots that faced Old Apex Road. During the auction, he hired a grading contractor to begin clearing and grading the street. He used the map to show the attendees where the street and the lots were located. The lots sold that day were barren and did not have a tree on them, but the sale brought in enough money for David to repay Mr. Powell and to have $4,000 left over to pay for grading and paving Marilyn Circle.

---

[31] Marilyn Circle was named, of course, for Marilyn Martin. David insisted that she, not movie star Marilyn Monroe, was the "real Marilyn."

CHAPTER 10

Triangle Forest

*Do you see someone skilled in their work? They
will serve before kings; they will not serve before
officials of low rank. (Proverbs 22:29 NIV)*

Whenever David could, he would take a course to sharpen and expand
his business skills. In the late 1950's, his experience while attending a
Dale Carnegie leadership course forever changed his outlook on work
and helped him focus on the business pursuits that would bring him the
most personal as well as monetary satisfaction. The class met at the First
Methodist Church in downtown Cary—in their annex, known as "The
Log Cabin." During the course, students were required to use the skills
they had been taught to deliver a professional speech to their classmates.
One evening, it was Jerry Miller's turn to deliver his speech.

*Jerry's Miller's speech about enjoying one's livelihood
changed David's perspective about work.*

A well-known Cary artist, who had first become acquainted with David as a customer of Martin's Cleaners, Jerry spoke about his passion for the work he did, which included drawing architectural designs for area builders. He also shared his outlook on work with the class. In the following story, he describes the night he made that speech and its effect on David: "I got up to speak one night and the instructor was from Duke University. I can't recall his name, but that night I had to get up there and talk about what I liked about what I did. I talked about drawing and architectural drawings and how much I really enjoyed doing all that, and I really put it on strong. I had a rolled-up newspaper and was just tamping the desk with it— with all my gestures, promoting myself as far as what I do, and I stressed in that talk that 'if you do not like what you do, quit and do something you really like to do. Don't be tied down to something that's dragging you down, but do what you like to do.'"

David listened intently. He was doing well in the car business, but hated what he was doing and was just about at wits end about what to do. Immediately after Jerry finished speaking, David stood up, faced the class and said that after hearing Mr. Miller's speech he was going to sell his car lot the next day and go into the building business! David's plan drew mixed reactions from the women in his life. David's mother was a bit concerned that he was leaving a business in which he had done so well, but Marilyn said she knew he would provide.

Euva Martin in June of 1958. David's mother was a bit concerned that he was leaving a business in which he had done so well.

She just went with the flow as he forged ahead with his new plans. David would later say that, without knowing it, Jerry had "saved his life that day." Up until that point, David's mindset regarding work had always been to put aside his desires and do whatever job or operate whichever business he could to meet his family's needs. After he heard Jerry's speech, being a good provider was still his goal, but he chose to do so through building projects or other business pursuits he thought he would enjoy. Jerry and David built a strong friendship after the course ended that remains until this day. In fact, the two became business associates. Jerry drew the plans for many of the houses and buildings David built or remodeled over the years. Later, after David built Cary's first mall, Jerry rented space for his business there. He even served for a time as President of the South Hills Merchants Association.

Jerry noted that David spent his time thinking and keeping notes in his pockets. "Marilyn, if she bought him a shirt—it had to have two pockets on it," Jerry recounted. "He would not wear a shirt that didn't have two pockets in it on the front of the shirt, and he keeps it full of notes. He's got a little book about two-and-a-half inches by five, and writes all his notes down. He writes them so small, I can't even hardly read it, and he always wants to know everybody."

Around this time David moved into the triplex he had built at 616 Chappell Drive in order to be closer to his ongoing work at University Apartments. The family began attending Boulevard Baptist Church in Raleigh. Over the years, that church has gone through a few name changes. It was previously named Jones Street Baptist Church and most recently Athens Drive Baptist Church. Donna recalled her parents led the singles ministry there and would hold cookouts for the group.

David did not just lead the singles ministry. He also took every opportunity he could to play Cupid, while teaching the young adults and attending church. "Daddy has always loved love," Donna recalled. "He set people up. He was always matchmaking. There are probably a lot of couples who are together because he set them up." David's interest in looking out for others' welfare also extended to helping widows or any other single person he knew, even if they were not fellow church members, find a spouse. He even played matchmaker for his family as it expanded. Martha and Joe Grissom were just the beginning. Of the many matches David has arranged, only one has ended in divorce! David was also a strong evangelical while he attended Boulevard Baptist

Church, and he still is! In fact, he would go out every Thursday night witnessing to people all over Raleigh, Cary, and beyond.

In 1959, while attending church he met Ray Cooke. A carpenter by trade, Ray and his wife, Lucille, had moved to Cary after he completed a two-year enlistment with the Army. He needed a job so he accepted a position with an area builder. However, his employer stopped building after a couple of months, and Ray was left without a job. "That was the hardest part of my life. When I was without work and I couldn't support my family," Ray said. Lucille had given birth to their first child right around the time he began working for the builder. In need of a job to support his family, he approached David about the possibility of working for him. "I knew Mr. Martin because he was very popular. I asked him for a job, and he said, 'yeah' immediately. I went to work for him two days before Christmas 1959. He gave me a turkey for Christmas, and I haven't been hungry since."

When Ray started working for David, they were building additional apartments on Chappell Drive as well as houses out at Triangle Forest. In 1961, David built a house for Ray and his family on Marilyn Circle.

Ray Cooke (in 2017) dressed in the type of clothes he normally wore when he worked for David.

David did two things that helped attract other prospective homeowners to Triangle Forest. First, he offered to build a house for his sister and brother-in-law, Martha and Joe Grissom. Mr. Grissom recalled the conversation he and David had about the house. "He came late one afternoon and said, 'Hey, this house is too small for your family and you have more children coming. I just bought a piece of land outside of Cary. I'll build you a house at cost out there, just to help get the place started, if you'll agree to move out there,'" Mr. Grissom said. "David really didn't need to offer us that kind of deal. He could have built a house out here and sold it anyway. But he wanted to help us—I know, and we've been out here ever since." Later, David also built a home in Triangle Forest for his cousin Jimmy Curl, this time on West Marilyn Circle.

Second, in March 1961 he advertised the sale of an "atomic house" complete with a reinforced bomb shelter. This advertisement caught the eye of area residents nervous about the possibility of nuclear war between the U.S. and the Soviet Union.

Since the end of World War II, the Soviets had acquired nuclear technology, and both countries had beefed up their nuclear arsenals in a frightening cycle of one-upmanship. As had already been demonstrated by the Korean conflict, this "Cold War" would continue as long as the Soviets persisted in forcing their ideology on the rest of the world, leaving the United States with no choice but to try to contain it. Tensions between the two governments reached a fevered pitch during the Cuban Missile Crisis in October 1962. The United States learned that the Soviets had placed nuclear missiles in Cuba, then under the control of the Communist dictator Fidel Castro. These missiles were located only 90 miles from the Florida coast and therefore capable of striking the U.S. mainland. President John F. Kennedy directed that U.S. Navy ships "quarantine" Cuba and prevent additional weapons from entering the country. After a tense 13-day standoff, what is now known as the Cuban Missile Crisis came to an end when President Kennedy and Soviet Premier Nikita Khrushchev came to an agreement leading to the removal of the missiles in Cuba as well as missiles in Turkey and Italy secretly deployed by the U.S. against the Soviet Union.[32] This crisis and the world situation in general only served to increase the attention generated by David's "atomic

---

[32] "Cuban Missile Crisis." History.com 4 Jan. 2010. Keyword: Cuban Missile Crisis.

house," spurred the construction of several more such structures, and prompted the beginning of the steady growth of Triangle Forest.

Meanwhile, David was also managing the transition from car lot owner to builder, and he had a lot of irons in the fire. One of the issues that arose was how he could attract more renters to University Apartments. He faced competition from the State College Apartment complex, built in the same area as his apartments, and there were quite a few other rental properties closer to the downtown area. Inspired by Marilyn, who had just learned to swim the year before, David decided he would install a pool for his tenants—something no other apartment complex in Raleigh offered at the time. The pool had its "grand opening" in June 1961. It was a big hit with tenants, many of whom decided to forgo vacation plans in favor of staying at home and enjoying their pool.

David, Sr., David, Jr., Donna, Dotty, and Marilyn

In fact, a significant number of them invited their out-of-town friends and relatives to visit and spend their vacation at University Apartments! The pool also provided a much-welcome recreational opportunity for stay-at-home moms and their kids. Before long David had rented all his units. In fact, the complex went five years without a vacancy. The cost of building the pool was never passed on to the tenants.[33]

David and his crew spent many hours working at the apartments, at Triangle Forest, and a new three-story office building they built at

---

[33] Meredith Council, "Build a Pool, Ideas for Apartment Owners," The Raleigh Times, 16 June 1961: Women's World, 10.

3700 Western Boulevard in Raleigh. With a gleam in his eye, Ray Cooke recalled that he and David were "go-getters" when it came to building projects. Ray estimated they built 30 houses in Triangle Forest alone. Over the years, David and his crew built houses in many other subdivisions in Cary and west Raleigh, including Hillsdale Forest, Roylene Acres, and Medfield Estates, just to name a few. Marilyn recalled that elderly residents in the area would call her on the telephone telling her David was working on a rooftop after dark. At one point, his service calls at the apartments began to interfere with his Sunday morning church attendance. This state of affairs continued until Sunday, February 15, 1961, when he went to a morning service and counted 35 women and seven men in one area of the Boulevard Baptist Church congregation. "The thought came to me, 'Where are the men?'" David recalled. "If it were not for the women leading us spiritually, America would be in bad shape." He promised God right then and there, he would not miss another Sunday morning service while he lived and was healthy enough to attend one. February 15, 2018, marked the 57th anniversary of his keeping his word to God. "If my church is closed because of inclement weather, I attend a Pentecostal Church, because they know who makes the ice," he said.

Life around David Martin during the 1960's could be described as one of movement and excitement. Besides being known as a man of conviction and a "go getter," one could also describe him as courageous and a defender of other's property, too. The following story he told illustrates this point: At about 11 o'clock one night, after David left the construction site at his 3700 Western Blvd property, on the corner of Gorman Street, he decided to stop and buy something to eat at a nearby convenience store. This store was located near the corner of Gorman Street and Western Blvd., across the street from the future location of a Wendy's fast-food restaurant. When David got to the store, he parked his car in the parking area and started to walk inside. At that very moment, a man ran out of the front door, with the store manager hot on his heels. David recalled: "The manager came out behind him and was pointing at the man. He yelled, 'Stop him! Stop him! He robbed us.' He'd robbed them of money. And the man had run across the Wendy's side across the street and then he doubled back. I had gotten out to try to grab him, but he ran across the street. When he did, he hit the curbing in front of the convenience store and turned a summersault. He got up and ran. After that, I jumped out of my car and opened the trunk and got my 12-gauge shotgun. Then I got back in and drove in his direction. I knew at that time that street was a dead end about two or three blocks away, so I figured he'd run between the houses that were just beyond the convenience store. He did, but I figured a get-a-way car must also be down there somewhere, so I went looking for it. I went down to the end of the street. I didn't see anything suspicious, and I came back. But coming back there was a car coming down Sherman Street, with its lights off that turned right onto Carlton Street and continued down that street. So, I whirled around, and I was driving wide open to catch him. I turned my flashers on and left them that way and turned my lights on and off to try to get him to stop. I knew he had to turn left and when I saw the get-a-way car do that I moved in fast to block him. Finally, I got him idled and stopped, and I held him there with my shotgun until the police arrived. In just a few moments there were five police cars there, and nobody ever complained about me being out there with my shotgun. They were appreciative that I caught the man. He was the get-away driver."

CHAPTER 11

A Vision Becomes a Reality

Where there is no vision, the people perish, but he that keepeth the law, happy is he. (Proverbs 29:18 NIV)

It seems reasonable to say that God blessed David's decision-making, his generosity and his faith in many ways. Mr. Martin recounted how the advice his friend and mentor, Raymond Morgan, gave him resulted in a blessing. He planted the idea in David's mind that he should be the one to build the first shopping center in Cary. After a Sunday service at First Baptist Church in Cary, Mr. Morgan, who was the manager of the local Hudson Belk department store in downtown Raleigh as well as a deacon at the church, called David over to where he was standing under a shade tree and said, "David, Cary is beginning to grow. One of these days somebody is going to build a shopping center out here. Have you ever thought about it?"[34] David had not, but their talk inspired him. He asked one of his tenants at University Apartments, Jerry Turner, if he could borrow some of his textbooks. At the time, Mr. Turner was attending North Carolina State College and majoring in landscape architecture. Later, he founded the architectural firm Jerry Turner and Associates and became a prolific planner and designer. As for David, he soaked up the material Mr. Turner lent him and anything else he could find on the subject. "I read everything I could get my hands on about shopping centers because I didn't know anything about them," David said. At first, he considered building his mall on land off Old Apex Road. However,

---

[34] Peggy Van Scoyoc, "Digitally Recorded Interview with David J. Martin," Sr. 28 Sep. 2010, 3.

he learned from the books Mr. Turner lent him that malls grow best when built near a thoroughfare. On a Sunday afternoon drive, not long after reading those books, he saw a for-sale sign on farmland along Buck Jones Road. "It fit the textbook description of what I needed: visibility and accessibility." The land, on the border of Raleigh and Cary, NC, was adjacent to U.S. Highway #1, then under construction.

Joe Grissom recalled that one day, while he and David were driving down Buck Jones Road, they passed the farmland. David told him that he planned to build a regional outlet mall on the land. Joe asked him if he had the money to purchase it. David said he was working on it, so Joe simply shrugged off the remark as just talk and forgot about it. David did purchase the land, however. He paid $110,000 at 4.5 percent interest for 78 acres, roughly $1,400 per acre or 3 cents per square foot.[35]

Initially, the land was in Raleigh's planning jurisdiction and could have been annexed by the city. A young Raleigh city councilman named Jesse Helms, who would go on to become an influential Republican U.S. Senator from North Carolina as well as an icon of the modern American conservative movement, helped David get the land rezoned to allow a shopping center there. However, the Raleigh Planning Commission and the City Council would not approve the rezoning all at once. They insisted on doing so in a piece-meal fashion. As a result, the "mall" was built in stages and has gone through several name changes over the years. During the first phase of construction, the property was named Southland Shopping Center. Construction began in 1961 and was completed in November 1963.[36]

The shopping center included a small grocery store, the Kwik Pik, which was run by Mrs. Lillie Hamrick Broadwell, David's mother-in-law. He built the store specifically with her in mind, so she would have a way to earn money after her husband passed away. She was an industrious woman and set up her sewing machine so that when she had some "down time" between customers she could sew for herself and her family. The center also included Southland Texaco, the Triangle's first self-service gas station.

---

[35] Chris Hubbard, "Profile David Martin," The Cary News, 26 Sept. 1998, pg. 4 B.
[36] The Cary News Editors, "Southland Shopping Center Grand Opening Today," The Cary News, 13 Nov. 1963, 1+

Southland Texaco pictured in a Raleigh Times news
story announcing its opening to the public.

The Texaco boasted a garage for car repairs, an air-conditioned lounge, restrooms, and a glass-enclosed office, which was next to the gas pumps. From there, the manager, Curtis Sauls, could be readily available to customers. The station also included a canopy and piped air to keep customers cool during the summer while their vehicles were serviced.[37] Housed in the basement of the same building was Gino's, an Italian restaurant that sold the first pizzas in Cary. One interesting feature of the restaurant was the Texaco mechanics' hydraulic lift, which extended into Gino's space in the basement, forcing the wait staff to work around it! Even before the first portion of Southland Shopping Center was completed, David had already made plans to enlarge it and transform it into an outlet mall.

David and Marilyn's business holdings were not the only thing that was expanding; so was their family. In February 1962, while they were still living in Raleigh, they welcomed the birth of their fourth child, Dale.

---

[37] The Cary News Editors. "Southland Shopping Center Grand Opening Today," The Cary News, Nov. 13, 1963, 1.

Dale when she was a toddler.

The earliest memory Dale has of her dad occurred when she was about three years old. It was Christmas time, and Marilyn took her and the three older children to her dad's building at 3700 Western Boulevard. "Santa Claus was in the parking lot," she recalled. "I was really excited. Then I looked down and said, 'This Santa Claus has my dad's hands.'"

Her sister Diane, hot on her trail, was born in October 1963. David recalls: "I called my mother and told her how Marilyn was having regular pains. I had gotten out some clothing and told her we needed to go to the hospital even though the labor pains were less severe than what she had experienced in the past. Marilyn insisted that the pains were caused by something she had eaten at the NC State Fair and declined to go. When I described the pains to my mother, she said, 'Son, that is not something she has eaten. Take her to the hospital!' I did, and it was the quickest delivery Marilyn had ever experienced." Marilyn remembers that she was in labor for only two hours before Diane was born. She loudly complained to David on the trip to Rex Hospital that the ride was too bumpy!

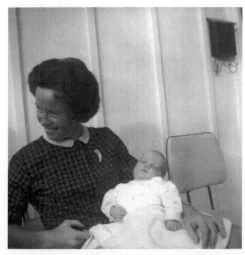

Marilyn holding Diane when she was an infant.

Diane was the only other child for whom David had a nickname. One of her early memories of him occurred while they drove together looking at some of his business sites. "We would be riding down the road and the sun would be reflecting and shining on my hair. So he said I was his 'heavenly sunshine,'" she recalled. "And the reason behind that was the other children—the girls—had straight hair and darker hair, but I had blonde hair and curls."

But Diane's, and really all her sisters', most treasured memory with their father was of the times he prayed for or with them. "The biggest thing for me was, any time we were going through anything, or mainly if we were hurt or if we were sick, the first person I would go to would be my dad because I knew he was going to come in and pray over me," she said. She added that they would hold hands, and sometimes he anointed them with oil when he prayed over them.

CHAPTER 12

Selling the Vision

And do not forget to do good and to share with others, for with such sacrifices God is pleased. (Hebrews 13:16 NIV)

One might have a great idea, but it takes other people to spread the message about it and to help make it a reality. Looking back on that time, David realized that God brought several people into his life to become his employees and help him spread his vision for South Hills Mall. Among them was a young woman named Joyce Hawley. She first came to work for him in a public relations role and later served as his leasing agent from the mid-1960's to the early 1970's. Before David met Joyce, she was very poor and lived in the country with her two young girls and her husband. The Hawleys did not have enough money to take their children, ages two and four, to see the doctor. Joyce made all their girls' clothing and grew whatever she could in her garden so they could eat. Eventually, she became so frustrated with their circumstances that she took a job with the Manpower employment agency selling Champion Maps. The maps were very popular in the U.S. during that period. Every five years the company published updated copies. Manpower paid an hourly wage and usually hired men to sell the maps, but the manager could not find a man to do the job. Having heard Joyce was qualified for the position, he called her in for an interview and hired her. When Joyce came aboard, Manpower had already renewed subscriptions with Champion's previous customers who wanted an updated map. Her job was to approach the customers who declined to renew their subscriptions and persuade them to reconsider. The company wanted to pay her $10 a day, but having found a babysitter who charged $6 a day, she told the manager she would accept the job on the condition that she was paid $6 a day plus a 20 percent commission on everything she sold. "They told me they would do that, but the first texa-cloth map I sold had to be free—no commission on that. They sold for $39.95 each. So, I got out and I started walking, and I walked all over Raleigh. I wasn't doing good because I couldn't figure out who needed this map. And the first week I scored very little, but one of the people I went to see was David Martin." Not only did David purchase the map from her, but he also asked her questions about her life. He learned that she had not had much luck drumming up business even after two weeks of work. In addition, she had been stuck in an elevator in downtown Raleigh's Wachovia building, and she had experienced all kinds of setbacks trying to sell the maps. David took time out of his busy schedule to sit down with her and help her think through what markets she should target. Joyce recalled: "He said, 'You ought to go see people that have trucks and service stations, where people have to give them out, and you need to go to service businesses.' He was the first person that was kind and took some time with me. So, I liked him, and the bottom line was in six weeks, I sold more of those maps than anybody had ever sold. And I made over $1,000, which was a lot of money." That money allowed her to buy things for her family they had never had before. "I bought my girls brand new dresses, and I bought my husband two suits from the Currins clothing store over in Fuquay-Varina—he hadn't had a suit since I met him—and I bought my family other clothes too. I even bought myself a couple of dresses for church."

Having tasted success selling the maps, Joyce said she was determined to continue earning money for her family. She was mulling over ideas about how she could do so when David called her. He asked her to come to his office so he could talk to her. When she did, he offered her a job working for him as his public relations, or PR, person.

Joyce Hawley, former South Hills PR associate and leasing associate.

Joyce had never heard of a PR person and asked him what the job would entail. David said her duties would include meeting and greeting prospective tenants when they came to the mall construction site as well as selling them on the location and how it would benefit them as the area grew. Part of her job included introducing herself to prospective tenants in other cities and informing them of the business opportunities the mall held. "I think I was only going to work like three days, and he was going to pay me $75, but I was only working limited hours because of my girls." Three days turned into a few weeks and then David took Joyce to the mall site. In what she said reminded her of Martin Luther King's "I Have a Dream," speech, he laid out in greater detail his plans. He told her his plan was to build a one-story, outlet mall, with entrances and exits at both ends of the structure, and he wanted it filled with a good tenant mix. Then he told Joyce he wanted her to be his leasing agent and promised her a salary of $150 a week.

One of the signs used to attract new tenants to South Hills Shopping Center.

He added that he just wanted her to go get the job done. If the weather was bad or her children were sick, she did not have to come to work. He also offered her a $500 bonus for every lease she secured, which sounded like a lot of money to her at the time. Despite not having any experience leasing space for a mall, she accepted the job. "I didn't know I wasn't supposed to do it like that, so I just went and did it, despite not having the tools I needed," she said.

Joyce, who also worked for years as a night club singer, appreciated David's fairness in offering her a flexible schedule. But there was one other even more important characteristic that distinguished him from all the other bosses she had before him. She explained: "Being a night club singer, as a young woman you had to fight off mangers and powerful men all the time. David Martin was probably the one true-blue boss I had. He was so religious. He always made sure there was no sign of impropriety about him, and he truly loved his wife."

Cary had only about 4,200 residents when Joyce began pitching the mall to prospective tenants. However, David had convinced her that the site he chose to build on was the best interchange between Atlanta and Washington, DC, because Interstate 40 as well as U.S. Highways #1 and #64 would eventually converge next to where he planned to build the mall. "So I had something to sell, and I believed in him," Joyce said. "So I went to the chamber of commerce, and I got aerial maps of everything. I made copies of it, massive copies of it, 50 copies of everything. I stapled it all together just like it was a beautiful brochure." Even though Joyce may not have had professionally printed materials to work with, pure enthusiasm for the project and the need to help provide for her family spurred her on. Each day she put on one of the new dresses and the high heels she had purchased with that Manpower check and would set out 50 miles in one direction one day and 50 miles in the opposite direction the next. "I went into those towns, with my little cute self, and I just walked the streets. I said, 'My name is Joyce Hawley and I'm from South Hills Mall,' and they couldn't resist talking to me. I would tell them, 'I'm representing South Hills Shopping Center at the best intersection in the South, and we are going to have a shopping center like no other shopping center.' I would tell them all about it and would say, 'We'd love for you to come see us.' I would leave them information and would come to see them so much I would just annoy them to death." She added, "I had a little flash camera that David bought me so that I could take pictures. If

I saw a shop that had a beautiful front to it, I took a picture and either kept it or gave it to David—when the time was right. We needed to know how to fix the front of a shop, and he could usually duplicate what he saw." Eventually, many of these prospective tenants came to see the construction site and to talk to David.

Prospective tenants were not the only people who came out to see what David was building; future business competitors did, too. Robert McAuliffe, Sr, who had 40 years of shopping center leasing experience and his son, Robert "Bob," McAuliffe, Jr, who was also in the business came to visit the site. The elder McAuliffe was associated with Crabtree Valley Mall, which was developed by Sam Longiotti, and eventually opened in 1972. Located in Raleigh, Crabtree is about nine miles away from South Hills, at the intersection of Glenwood Avenue, which is also U.S. Hwy 70 and N.C. Hwy 50, and the I-440 Beltline. The younger McAuliffe eventually befriended and mentored her. "And he ended up telling me everything I needed to know, over a period of time," Joyce said. "I had to learn to figure out square footage and all that stuff. He would say, 'That ain't the way you do it Joyce! That is not the way you do it!' Well he would talk and I had my little notebook and I'd take it down real fast—what I was supposed to do." Wisely following her boss's example, Joyce learned all she could from any source possible and wrote it down. Despite the help Joyce received from some people others in the business community were not very congenial and laughed at or made fun of her efforts on behalf of the mall, but she and David pressed onward.

Bob Jr. told Joyce about the annual conferences of the International Council of Shopping Centers (ICSC) and how beneficial these meetings were for mall leasing agents. The ICSC works to advance the shopping industry and to promote its role in the commercial distribution of goods and services. At these conferences, events are held to allow owners, developers, retailers, brokers, lenders, municipalities, and property asset managers as well as product and service providers to exhibit their properties, make deals, and form successful business partnerships. Joyce recalled the occasion when she told David how helpful it would be if she attended one of these conferences: "I said, 'I need to go to an ICSC convention, David, and I've got to fly in there. I've got to stay in a hotel, and I've got to rub noses with all these people.'" He agreed and sent her to her first one, in Miami. "The first one I went to, it was me and 7,200 men. I stayed in the Mayview Hotel, and I was ignorant." Eventually, the time David allowed her to network paid off. "That's where I got Butler Shoes. I got a couple of national tenants," she said.

Whenever there was a lull in the planning and construction process for the mall, David and his crew continued work on Triangle Forest. Home sales were slow, and the prices were low until he received a little help in 1965 from International Business Machines (IBM) executives who decided to build a 400-acre, 600,000-square-foot research facility in the Research Triangle Park (RTP). According to the Learn NC website, "The RTP was founded by a committee of government, university and business leaders as a model for research, innovation, and economic development." By establishing the park, "the founders hoped to improve the economic conditions in the region between Durham, Raleigh and Chapel Hill, and to increase the employment opportunities for the citizens of North Carolina." [38] Their plan worked for David. When IBM's employees and their families moved to the area, they needed housing, and Triangle Forest helped fulfill their needs. David said, "When IBM moved in the prices shot up."

Not everyone was happy with the way the region and Cary were being affected by the RTP and the businesses that moved into or near it. Some of David's friends took the attitude of, "Yankee go home," but not David. "My mother taught me to show appreciation for people that help you out," he said. "My friends from up north came down here and brought the home values up. I love them for coming and helping me. You don't bite the hand that feeds you."

[38] "Research Triangle Park: Evolution and Renaissance," Rick L. Weddle, et al NC Pedia, Keyword: Research Triangle Park, 2006.

CHAPTER 13

Community Activism

Then He said to them, "Then render to Caesar
the things that are Caesar's; and to God the things
that are God's." (Matthew 22:21 NIV)

David's enthusiasm for growth did not mean he lacked concern for his community. While others voiced their concerns or outright complained about the growth in the region, David had already taken a more proactive approach. He joined a government watchdog group, The Wake County Taxpayers Association.

This political action committee, which had a conservative slant, was founded on October 23, 1962, at the suggestion of the tax committees of the Raleigh Merchants' Bureau, the Raleigh Chamber of Commerce, and the Raleigh Board of Realtors.[39] Their mission was to give taxpayers a voice on how their tax dollars were spent; to encourage them to become better informed about the work of the county's departments; to promote sound and practical city and county budgeting; to encourage taxpayers to control their desire for government spending; and to urge taxing policies that would not burden citizens.[40] It was comprised of elected officers and a board of directors—15 of whom represented the city of Raleigh, and one director representing each of the other municipal governments in the county. The group's Raleigh directors led

---

[39] Charles Craven. "Wake Taxpayers Group formed: Goals Outlined," <u>The Raleigh Times</u>, 23 Oct. 1962, 1.
[40] Charles Craven, "Wake Taxpayers Group formed: Goals Outlined," <u>The Raleigh Times</u>, 23 Oct. 1962, 1.

committees that studied the work done and money spent by each of the City of Raleigh's departments. They did the same thing for other, smaller towns in the county. The county directors, which were comprised of representatives from Raleigh and the remaining towns in Wake County, studied the county government's departments and, during the budgeting process, recommended ways county officials could save money or offer services more efficiently.[41] The group also held meetings and invited officials from Raleigh, the other towns, and the county to speak about the problems they faced finding revenue for necessary projects. They also advocated for the merger of the Raleigh and Wake County School Districts. In order to maintain the economic strength of the county, they sought the revaluation of properties.[42] In addition, they fought to ensure that late penalty fees for taxes were returned to citizens who had not received their tax bills in time.[43] Prominent men from across the county who helped form the group included the former Mayor of Raleigh, James E. Briggs, who served as the group's first president; Wesley Williams, the former executive secretary of the Raleigh Merchants Bureau, and W.T. Cooper, David's longtime friend, who served as a director representing Cary.[44] David served two terms as the president of the group and at least one term on the board of directors. The group's membership dwindled as the original members aged or went on to other pursuits, but the name "Wake County Taxpayers Association" would again be used decades later to promote the agenda of conservatives in Wake County.

While David was busy developing Triangle Forest and pursuing his dream of building a regional mall, he and Marilyn laid the last shingle in their family, so to speak, when she became pregnant with their youngest child, a daughter. Debbie was born in May 1967 and was the only one of the Martin siblings whose birth was specifically planned by their parents.

---

[41] The Raleigh Times Editors. "Taxpayers Group Elects Leaders," The Raleigh Times, 20 Feb.1963, 1.

[42] The News and Observer Editors. "City, Wake Money Problems Discussed," The News and Observer, 10 Jan. 1969.

[43] "Citizens Group Urges Tax Penalty Refunds," The News and Observer, 20 Feb. 1963, 24.

[44] The Raleigh Times Editors, Taxpayers Group Elects Leaders," The Raleigh Times 20 Feb.1963.

Debbie with her proud parents Marilyn and David, Sr.

She was born after David and Marilyn had tried for three years to have another child. By the time she arrived, the family had moved into a home in Triangle Forest at 103 Marilyn Circle. Debbie would help provide one of her sister Diane's earliest memories of their dad. "Mom had gone out one evening, and Dad cut Debbie's hair because it was in her eyes. When Mom came home, of course, she was mortified because her bangs were very short and crooked. He didn't do a very good job." A few years prior, his children's pony had hair in its eyes, and David had mangled its bangs too!

David with his children's pony, Cracker Jack, after he cut its bangs.

78

Debbie's earliest memories of her Dad are a collage of different times she held his hand. Many of her memories are from the time spent with the family on vacation at Myrtle Beach. "Whenever he was around I was very proud—very happy, and I felt very safe," she said. "It would be exciting to have him there, even if it wasn't a lot of time." She also remembered one of the first times she felt protective of her Dad. "He had come to Myrtle Beach and had put on shorts with his Sunday shoes and black socks.

David wearing the black socks as he did in Debbie's story.

He looked comical, and even some of my sisters were embarrassed for him, but he was my Dad and I felt proud. I got so mad because these drunk teenagers were laughing at him and his white legs," she laughed. "And it was like, 'How dare you laugh at my father!'"

When Debbie was a little older, David let the Cary Jaycees use a portion of South Hills Mall for one of their fundraisers. It was close to Halloween so the Jaycees decided they would raise money by charging admission for people to walk through a haunted house they had set up. David then decided to go a step further in his support of the Jaycees. He purchased tickets to the haunted house for Debbie, Dale, Diane, and himself. The day of the event David was, as always, holding Debbie's hand while they walked through the mall. Before they could reach the trail leading to the house, Dale took off running and refused to go any further. Undeterred, David, Debbie, and Diane continued walking toward the haunted house. When they came to the starting point, Diane noticed a "dead bride" lying in a coffin. It scared her so much that she too ran away and would not come near the house. That left just Debbie and her father to walk alone through the house. Debbie described the rest of her experience. "I prayed the entire time, but I was safe because I was with my Dad. When we got out of the haunted house, Dad was still holding my hand. I said, 'I made it through Lord, you can turn me loose now!' My Dad responded, 'He never turns us loose. He always stays with us.' I just remember what a great feeling that was. I made it through with the help of my Dad and my Big Dad!"

CHAPTER 14

Developing South Hills

*All hard work brings a profit, but mere talk leads
only to poverty. (Proverbs 14:23 NIV)*

Back at home, construction on what David had now decided to call South
Hills Shopping Center continued. Later that year, the bank building
was completed. It would eventually house the Carolina Bank and later
Central Carolina Bank (CCB), which eventually became SunTrust Bank.

The South Hills Bank building as it looked in 2006.

A brief interaction between David and his masonry contractor
during the construction of that building would lead to the following
anecdote: Apparently, David, who was then about 40 years old, needed
to hitch a very large steel trailer—it had a five-inch square tongue—to

his tractor. He asked his brick mason, a burly 250-pound man, to do it. However, when the man reached down to grab the tongue it would not budge. David, a mere 5 feet, 8 inches and weighing only 160 pounds, decided to take a turn at it and jumped down from the tractor. To the amazement of the brick mason, David picked up the trailer hitch with one hand and attached it to the tractor. For years, still filled with awe at this display of strength, the brick mason told that story, and David's family members still tell it today.

In the mid-1960s David and his crew started gathering bricks from various demolition projects for which they had been hired. David planned to use these bricks to construct the South Hills Service Plaza. The state paid him to demolish the old boarding school dormitory at Cary High School, located at the corner of Dry Avenue and Faculty Drive. He was also contracted—privately—to tear down the old Calvary Baptist Church next to Memorial Auditorium in Raleigh. Some of the bricks used to construct the plaza and later the inside of the mall came from bricks handmade about 150 years prior by inmates at Raleigh's Central Prison. In addition, he obtained brick from the demolition of buildings in what is now Raleigh's Dix Hill Historic District. His friend Jerry Miller recalled seeing David and his workers—some of them teen-aged boys—sitting day after day, for hours, in the hot sun chucking the mortar off the bricks with a trowel. Ray Cooke added that besides giving the boys an opportunity to earn some money, one of the reasons David offered them jobs was to keep them from getting into trouble!

Work on the two-level service plaza, just over 50,000 square feet in size, was completed in 1969. The Furniture Gallery, on the upper level, and the Winn-Dixie grocery, on the lower level, were among the first two stores to lease space. In fact, the story of how the Winn-Dixie Corporation made the decision to rent space at South Hills is a great example of how "networking" benefited David. It also illustrates how David impressed others with his involvement in every aspect of his business. The story begins with Jerry Miller's brother, A.K. Miller, the owner of A.K. Miller Heating and Cooling in Goldston, NC. A.K.'s company was contracted to provide maintenance services for the Winn-Dixie Corporation's newly constructed grocery stores. Later A.K. told Joe Joy, the Winn-Dixie executive in charge of new construction in the Triangle area, that his brother Jerry drew architectural designs. When Mr. Joy was in the area, he contacted Jerry, who had opened an office in the South Hills Plaza. The two discussed the services Jerry could provide Winn-Dixie. As a result, Mr. Joy hired Jerry to draw building plans for the grocery chain. After Jerry had worked for Winn-Dixie for a while, Mr. Joy came to see him and asked him if he knew David Martin. Mr. Joy wanted to rent space for one of the company's stores at South Hills Shopping Center. Jerry recalled what he told him: "I said, 'Right now you can't see him. He's below the ground.' He couldn't believe it. David was in a hole putting in pipes and so forth. Now he was the guy who owned the shopping center. He was down in the hole digging. It was nothing to see him always out there on his grader or a great big bulldozer. He was always out there cleaning his parking lot. Mr. Joy thought David Martin was a man with a suit who sat in his office all day. But not David Martin. He worked. He wasn't going to tell somebody to do something unless he was willing to get down and do it."

Other businesses or eateries which have called the South Hills Plaza home at different times, just to name a few, have included: Austin Food Snack Outlet, Betty Kovach Dance studio, Cary Kennel Supply, Glenda's Beauty Shop, Ideal Cleaners, Karate U.S.A., Life Experiences, Overton's, Peking Inn Restaurant, R.P. Construction, Stereo Trends, South Hills Barber Shop, South Hills Coin Laundry, and the South Hills Shoe Shop.

CHAPTER 15

Incident on Rhamkatte Road

*Blessed are the peacemakers, for they will be
called children of God. (Matthew 5:9 NIV)*

The year 1969 was memorable for the Martins and their children
not only because the construction at South Hills Shopping Center
was going full-steam ahead but also because that year marked the
occurrence of the most frightening event the Martins ever endured.
On Sunday, October 12, 1969, after attending services at Boulevard
Baptist Church, David and Marilyn loaded their children into the
family station wagon so they could visit her mother in New Hill,
NC. Around 1 p.m., David was driving east of Holly Springs, NC,
on Rhamkatte Road—now known as Holly Springs Road—when a
highway patrolman flagged him down. David noticed that a crowd of
around 35-50 African-Americans had gathered around a basketball
court watching Trooper John Pittman, a North Carolina highway
patrolman, struggle to arrest Octavius "Red Horse" Norris. According
to the Raleigh *News and Observer* and the *Raleigh Times* newspapers,
the trooper had pulled Mr. Norris over because the car he was driving
was an unregistered automobile displaying a license plate belonging
to another vehicle.[45] David stopped to assist the trooper and parked
the station wagon at an angle in the roadside ditch. As he got out of
the car, he instructed Marilyn to back it up and park it on the road.
The altercation became so violent that, after she had backed the car

---

[45] The Raleigh Times Editors. "Investigation Slated in Shooting Incident," The
Raleigh Times, 13 Oct. 1969, 1.

onto the road, she froze where she was. "I think I was in a state of shock," Marilyn recalled. What David did not know was that during an attempt to arrest Norris the previous year, an altercation ensued, and Trooper Pittman broke the man's jaw with his blackjack. To make matters worse, Norris was under the influence of alcohol when David happened upon the altercation, and the big man was known to become violent when he drank too much. When David walked over to where the scuffle between Pittman and Norris was under way, the officer asked David to follow him to the jail. David agreed to help, and Norris calmed down enough to allow himself to be taken into custody. David shared the following about what happened next: "Mr. Norris agreed to go with Trooper Pittman, and he walked around to the passenger side of the patrol car. The patrolman put him in the front seat instead of the back seat—that was kind of crazy—and closed his door. But he still wanted me to follow them in. Mr. Norris changed his mind and tried to escape by jumping out on the side of the steering wheel before that officer could get around the patrol car and into the driver's seat. So they started fighting again. They fought around the car out of my sight, but my wife and children saw the continued fighting."

David wanted to help calm the situation, but he lost sight of what occurred between Norris and Pittman because three of the men who had gathered to watch the fight barred his way. "They stopped me, and said they weren't going to let us double-team Red Horse." David finally convinced them to let him by, but not before Marilyn and the rest of the family witnessed a bloody fight that scared them and left a permanent memory etched in the older children's minds. The two men fought in front of and around the house with the basketball court in the background. At one point, Norris took Trooper Pittman's blackjack, beat him on the head with it, threw him to the ground and tried to choke him. Pittman in turn grabbed his .357 Magnum and shot Mr. Norris in the chest.[46] When David got to the scene where the shooting occurred, he heard the injured man ask the trooper, 'Why you shoot me?' At that point, David tried to get someone from the crowd to take Norris to the hospital because he was afraid to leave Trooper Pittman. Since no one volunteered to help, David told his children to move to the back of

[46] The Raleigh Times Editors. "Investigation Slated in Shooting Incident," Raleigh Times, 13 Oct. 1969, 1.

the station wagon so he could transport Norris himself. David did not realize, however, that when Norris had tried to escape, Trooper Pittman had immediately called for back-up. Two additional Highway Patrol cars and two Wake County Sheriff's office vehicles arrived before David and his family could leave with Norris. When David saw them, he helped persuade Norris to let the officers take him to the hospital.

> **"I put my hands on him and talked him into going with the police," David said. "I was close enough that he could have hit me, or I could have hit him. But I was a peacemaker. In other words I got him convinced that he ought to go."**
>
> **–David J. Martin, Sr.**

"Then as he started that way another patrolman showed up. Mr. Norris knew the other patrolman and had respect for him. When he saw that other patrolman, he was ready to go. He was satisfied that he'd be treated right."

The day after the incident, *The News and Observer* and *The Raleigh Times* reported that the other patrolmen took Mr. Norris and Trooper Pittman to the hospital, where the officer was released after treatment for bruises, a bump on his head, and a swollen throat. The papers reported that Mr. Norris was in satisfactory condition.[47] Perhaps to protect the Martins from any unwanted publicity as well as to ease tensions between the police and the African-American community, neither *The News and Observer* nor *The Raleigh Times* mentioned they had witnessed the altercation.[48] Nothing was written about other significant details concerning the confrontation either. At the time of the incident, tensions were high in some areas of the state, such as in Sanford, NC, where the African-American community and the police were at odds over disturbances stemming from civil rights and other societal issues. It

[47] News and Observer Editors. "Patrolman Shoots Man in Scuffle," News and Observer, 13 Oct. 1969, 1.
[48] News and Observer Editors, "Patrolman Shoots Man in Scuffle," The News and Observer, 13 Oct. 1969, 1. and The Raleigh Times Editors. "Investigation Slated in Shooting Incident, The Raleigh Times, 13 Oct. 1969, 1.

also was not in David's character to mention ways in which he helped people or tried to ease tensions in situations. He did receive a letter from NC Patrol Captain John T. Jenkins dated October 23, 1969, expressing appreciation for his coming to the aid of Trooper Pittman. The letter commended David for his efforts and stated that the North Carolina Highway Patrol felt that David's presence helped keep the situation from becoming more serious and they were aware he could have been injured while he was there.

David Jr., who was 13 at the time of the altercation, and Donna, who was 12, were scheduled to testify in court about what they witnessed that day. Some months later, prepared to testify, they arrived at the Wake County Courthouse but were never called to the witness stand.

CHAPTER 16

Deepening Cary Roots

Whoever can be trusted with very little can be trusted with much. (Luke 16:10 NIV)

Happier times followed in 1970 when the Martins started attending First Baptist Church in Cary, where David had worshipped as a boy with his mother and siblings. Before long, David and Marilyn became close friends with the pastor, Dr. Harvey Duke, and his wife, June. Besides their great love for God, it was easy to see why the couples became close. Both men had the best interest of the congregation in mind and gave their hearts, minds, soul and strength to endeavors they thought would help or advance First Baptist's goal of honoring God. Both had served their country at sea—Dr. Duke was a retired Navy captain—and their wives dutifully supported them. Additionally, their children were roughly the same age, attended youth group activities together, and were close to the leaders of those groups. After services concluded on Sunday morning, the two families could often be seen having lunch together at the Burger King on Hillsborough Street in Raleigh. David also invited families who visited First Baptist Church on Sundays out to eat with his family in order to get to know them better and to witness to them. He continues this practice, as well as a variety of other means of Christian witness, to this day!

As time went on, David was elected to the Board of Deacons. He has served at least six terms as a deacon at First Baptist since he and Marilyn officially joined the church in October, 1970. Mrs. Duke reminisced, "The deacons all had their little flocks to tend to.

*David and Dr. Duke on break from a Southern
Baptist Convention held in Indiana.*

They did this for four years and then took a break." David was known
for his benevolence to the groups he led and for his dedication to visiting
people who were sick or had missed church. Mrs. Duke also recalled
when people asked David for help, he would give them a job and have
them cut the grass or perform other tasks around the church. "He gave
them the means to help themselves," Mrs. Duke said. Even when David
was no longer serving on the deacon board, he continued to support
the church in various capacities, only some of which were known to his
fellow church members. Just as often, he would become involved behind
the scenes on issues of concern within the church. Long-time members
of the church often called David if they felt something needed to change

in the church because they knew he had the character to do something about it.

When he wasn't at church, David was busy overseeing his various projects, including ongoing construction and leasing activity at South Hills. He reached an early milestone in his effort to transform Southland Shopping Center into South Hills Shopping Center when The Carolina Bank opened on November 30, 1970, in the newly-constructed bank building, later renamed the Reintgen Building. The bank offered complete banking services and featured three drive-up teller lanes. The fact that the building's entrance faced away from the street as well as the fact that the exit from its parking lot led into the larger South Hills lot, not directly onto Buck Jones Road, reflected the latest thinking in bank security at the time. These aspects of the building's design played a large part in attracting Carolina Bank, as well as successor tenants, Central Carolina Bank and SunTrust Bank, to this particular location at South Hills.

South Hills was not the only place where growth was occurring. In nearby Cary, during the period from 1970 to 1975, the population doubled from just over 7,000 people to a little over 14,000 people, spawning growth in the community's housing and infrastructure.[49] In order to highlight the growth and vitality of the town as well as honor its past, Cary held a Centennial Celebration the week of May 8-12, 1971. The Celebration marked the 100th anniversary of the town's founding. As part of the festivities, the town declared May 9, 1971, as Religious Heritage Day, which culminated in an ecumenical worship service at Cooper's Field. Several of the town churches contributed singers to a community choir formed especially for the occasion. The choir performed selections from Handel's "Messiah" during the service. Later in the week a 100-year time capsule was buried with the hope that in 2071 Cary citizens will to be able open it and see documents and mementos from the celebration.[50] David supported the event by joining a society who dubbed themselves "The Brothers of the Brush of Cary, NC." Members of the group agreed to do their civic duty and grow a moustache, full beard, goatee, or sideburns for the Centennial Celebration.

[49] Thomas M. Byrd, *Around and About Cary*, Edwards Brothers, Inc., Ann Arbor, MI, 1970, p. 87.
[50] Thomas M. Byrd, *Around and About Cary*, Edwards Brothers Inc., Ann Arbor, MI, 1970.

David as he dressed during the Cary Centennial Celebration.

They also agreed to wear a badge that designated them official boosters of the festivities and to wear a derby or top hat while participating in special events. In addition, they promoted and took part in Caravan Booster trips, historical tours of Cary. The rest of the Martin clan joined in the fun as well and were dressed in the same manner as the townspeople back in 1871.

David and Marilyn during the Cary Centennial Celebration.

David Jr. wore trousers and a shirt from that era. Marilyn and the girls wore long dresses. David Sr. took out an ad in the *Cary News* containing a photo of him in his suit, full beard, and long sideburns!

CHAPTER 17

Building the South Hills Community

*No one should seek their own good, but the good
of others. (I Corinthians 10:24 NIV)*

David always had a heart for people who were trying to follow God. He
was willing to work with area church leaders who wanted to construct
buildings for their congregation or needed a place to meet. Often, he
would help design their church buildings and, to save on labor costs,
would draw his workforce from that church's membership. In August
1970, he began work on a building for the Cary Church of Christ that
would seat 250 people.

*An August 1970 Raleigh Times newspaper photo of the groundbreaking
ceremony for the Cary Church of Christ building.*

He completed the project in April 1971. The church was at the corner of Walnut Street and Nottingham Drive, just around the corner from South Hills. It was later sold to the Point Church—which still occupies it—along with eight other locations in the Triangle area, at the time of this book's publication.

He also was hired to construct the White Plains Methodist Church and worked with that congregation on a few projects, including a parsonage. Ray Cooke said he and David assisted in the building of the churches, but the parishioners did most of the work. "It was difficult, but it was OK. We had to work with people who didn't know what they were doing, but we coached them along." David's work on churches impressed Jerry Miller: "One thing you won't get out of David Martin is him bragging about what he does. I know he has built churches for people that didn't have the money to do it."

The transformation of Southland Shopping Center into South Hills Mall and Plaza as well as the construction of several free-standing buildings occurred simultaneously with the construction of the Cary Church of Christ.

After completing the Plaza in 1969, David and his crew began work on the Happy Inn, between the Plaza and the service station. When completed in 1971, it was the first three-story hotel in Cary and later became home to a Motel 6. Construction was behind schedule, and the Happy Inn was almost not completed in time for a convention already scheduled there. David pulled Joyce Hawley and Clara O'Neil, who also worked in his office, away from their normal jobs and had them work alongside his male employees installing sheetrock in the building to help speed up the construction.

Construction of the South Hills Mall itself commenced, and even David Jr. and Donna were called on to help at the construction site at different times. Donna recalled they carried stop signs to direct traffic while her father and his men graded roads coming into the mall. On one occasion, her father got upset with David, Jr. because he placed Donna at the bottom of a hill, causing her to be covered in red dust from head to toe from the "good 'ole Carolina red clay" they were grading!

Everyone's hard work paid off when in 1972 the south portion of the mall was completed. Southland Shopping Center was renamed and advertised as South Hills Mall and Plaza. Ray Cooke recalled the arduous pace the work crew kept up to build the first phase and the sense of accomplishment they felt when it was complete: "This was an outlet mall, and we worked like crazy to get it opened before the Prime Outlet Mall opened in Morrisville, NC, which is about eight to 10 miles away from South Hills Mall—and we did," Ray Cooke recalled, with a chuckle. "We built the first outlet mall in the area." He added that the crew, which usually included about six men, would turn on their headlights after the sun went down so they could continue to work. Obviously, David's habit of working until "dark-thirty" was alive and well!

Opening week, in September 1972, David invited Reverend David McLaurin, then a 16-year-old evangelist, to preach at the mall. Rev. McLaurin was somewhat of a novelty at the time. He got his start at a youth-led Sunday service at Piney Grove Baptist Church, in Fuquay-Varina, NC, at age 14. He was licensed to preach when he was 15.

The *Fuquay-Varina Independent* weekly newspaper featured an article about his first service, and he began to get other offers to preach to youth in the area. When David heard about him, he contacted Piney Grove's minister, Rev. C. Paul Jones, who handled McLaurin's preaching schedule, and invited the young man to preach at the mall.

Opening day, when David's tenants began arriving at the mall, the corridors had been lined with large plaques depicting the crucifixion. Other images of Jesus, a large stage, and a full public-address system had also been installed inside. When the tenants inquired about the set-up, they learned that Rev. McLaurin was scheduled to speak there the entire week. They began to call David's leasing agent, Joyce Hawley, at home to complain. Joyce, who was getting her children ready for the day, was taken by surprise. She had planned for balloons, the Cary and Apex school bands to perform, and other activities normally associated with a mall opening, but had not been prepared for what amounted to a revival. She tried to dissuade David from going through with his plan, but he had made up his mind that his customers would hear from the Bible and learn about God that week. At different points in his sermon, the young minister boldly asked his audience and any passing customers to stop what they were doing to kneel and pray. But, despite tenants threatening to leave due to the preaching and religious decorations, Joyce could neither persuade David to discontinue the young preacher's sermons nor to remove the plaques from the mall's corridor. When interviewed by *The News and Observer*, David said he would rather listen to Rev. McLaurin preach than hear Billy Graham. He repeatedly invited the young minister back to preach at the mall.[51] In time, David also invited a gospel group from Fayetteville, NC, the Revelators, to perform with McLaurin.

As David has learned many times during his life, success does not come without some setbacks. A few months after the first phase of the mall was completed, David was notified that a fire had started in the carpet store there. He rushed to the scene to see what he could salvage. When he arrived Jim Matthews, the chief of the YRAC[52] Rural Fire Department, along with his crew had already arrived and were assessing the situation. They had responded to the call, though technically the South Hills area fell within the jurisdiction of the Cary Fire Department. The two departments always supported each other so the YRAC firemen worked until the Town of Cary folks arrived. Chief Matthews, grandson of the Martin Family's good friend and benefactor Lovie Matthews, recalled that when his trucks arrived he and his men found the carpet store engulfed in flames. Acrid smoke was pouring out of the space. The terrible smell came from the burning rubber and other synthetic materials used in the carpets and padding. The firemen were about to take out a large, fixed, plate-glass window, but David arrived minutes later saying he wanted to take it out. "Well, I was the fire chief, and I said, 'David we don't have the time to disassemble this. We have to get in there and get this smoke out before the building explodes.'" David repeated his request, and Chief Mathews said, "I'll give you about three minutes to get it out, and then we're going in whether the window is out or not." Matthews continued, "David went to work with a hammer and a pry bar. He had that window out in about two minutes and saved the window. But that's his nature. That window would have been expensive to replace whether insurance was a factor or not. That's the way he thinks. We got the fire out, saved the building, and saved the window."

David wasn't one to be slowed down by a little misfortune and soon afterward he announced his plan to build twin theaters across the street from the mall. Their seating capacity would be 350 people each. The theaters were franchised by Jerry Lewis Cinemas and had a joint office. According to *The Raleigh Times*, "Martin said the theaters will 'have

---

[51] Margie Davidson, "Teen Preacher Delivers message," The News and Observer, October, 1972.

[52] "YRAC" is "CARY" spelled backwards.

the cleanest movies in town. Every movie will have to be okayed by the National Council of Churches. Absolutely no X-rated movies will be shown.'" [53] When the South Hills Twin Theater opened in July, 1973, the opening movie was the Christian musical "Godspell." Several of David's children had jobs at the theater when they were teenagers. As David had promised, clean, family-oriented movies were the only movies that ever played there while he owned it.

During the same period, David started his practice of allowing the mall and outlying parcels to be used by churches for what he considered God's work. One of those churches was led by Doug Allen, a student at Southeastern Seminary and leader of the newly-formed Cary Church of God. David let the church hold services Sunday morning and evenings in the mall. "Then, after he built the motel next door, he moved us to a meeting room in its basement," Dr. Allen recalled. "And for all of that, he never charged us anything—which was a huge blessing." Impressed with the "Spirit-filled" nature of the Pentecostal church, David offered to construct a building for the congregation, but only if the membership would agree to affiliate with the Southern Baptist Convention, a move David thought would help the church grow faster. The church declined David's request, and later, after church members had erected their own building and their membership had grown quite a bit, the men saw each other again. David asked Rev. Allen why his church had problems. When Dr. Allen seemed surprised at this comment, David jokingly said, "Your church isn't supposed to grow like a Baptist church," and the two had a good laugh! Dr. Allen added the following about David: "He has been a great friend of mine and of the church. He has done quite well and is a very wealthy man, but he's always been a down-to-earth and positive person." In fact, when Dr. Allen met him for lunch years later in June 2017 and expressed a desire to come out of retirement to help build and grow churches, David enthusiastically encouraged him to do so.

Over the years, South Hills has served as a meeting place for many religious groups and an "incubator" of sorts for many local churches. Here is only a partial list of churches and religious organizations that either got their start at South Hills or leased space at South Hills during a critical period in their ministry: Cary Church of God, Community

---

[53] "New twin theaters planned," *The Raleigh Times*, September 15, 1972, Sec. A, P. 6, Col. 2.

Life Church (later renamed Sovereign Grace Church), New Life Church, Cornerstone Baptist Church, Women's Aglow, Christ Cathedral of Praise (later renamed Life Song Church). Several of these groups met in the Community Room, located in the mall next door to the locally famous seafood restaurant, Vicky's Calabash Pier. These groups shared that facility with other civic groups, such as the American Legion. No group was ever charged rent for the Community Room. The restaurant and the Community Room no longer exist as they were closed in 2003 to make way for mall renovations. However, David's tradition of supporting religious organizations continues. He has rented a suite of offices in the South Hills Plaza to various Christian ministries over the years, including Hope Community Church. Currently, this space is occupied by Hope Connection International, a non-profit Christian-based organization that assists people in the community impacted by abuse or addiction. David has also leased a retail space in the plaza to Hope Connection for a thrift shop, conveniently located only a few steps away from their office.

In the meantime, David continued to invite Rev. McLaurin to preach and either the Revelators or other local Christian groups to perform at the mall on Saturday nights, until the mid-1970s. The young minister also credited David with being instrumental in helping him acquire Cary Middle School as the venue for a Cary Youth Crusade. "David Martin had a tremendous influence on me as a young person, and his going out on a limb like he did for me was very meaningful to me," he said. The exposure he received at South Hills Mall also led to opportunities for him to preach at about 25 revivals a year—from Maryland to Florida— between 1974 and 1978, he explained. The mall holds a special place in his heart for another reason. It was there that he first met Sharon Powell, his wife since 1975.

Rev. McLaurin went on to major in religion at Campbell University and continued preaching. He later received his master's degree from Southwestern Baptist Theological Seminary in Fort Worth, Texas. During his successful career as an evangelist, he began to feel a call to pastoral ministry. His first pastorate was at Necessity Baptist Church in Caddo, Texas. Over the course of his career, McLaurin has served churches in North Carolina, South Carolina, Kentucky, and Florida. As this book goes to press, he has returned to his home state, serving as pastor of Duncan Baptist Church in northern Harnett County, NC.

CHAPTER 18

South Hills Challenges

Do not store up for yourselves treasures on earth, where
moths and vermin destroy, and where thieves break in
and steal. But store up for yourselves treasures in heaven,
where moths and vermin do not destroy, and where thieves
do not break in and steal. For where your treasure is,
there your heart will be also. (Matthew 6:19-21 NIV)

David strove to hold fast to his guiding "J.O.Y. Principle—Jesus First, Others Second, Yourself Last." This philosophy applied to his family, friends, business associates, and total strangers alike.

As many of David's friends already did, Joyce came to know that David's success did not come *in spite of* his applying Christian principles to his business dealings but actually *because of* his choosing to do the right thing. Despite David passing up what seemed to Joyce to be major opportunities, with God's help, David compiled a very respectable tenant mix, including several regional and national retailers.

'AVID MARTIN (right) developer of South Hills hopping Center, smiles happily as T. B. Rose, Jr. enter) cuts the ribbon to mark the opening of oses Store last week. In addition to Roses, three

other stores, Kerr Rexall, Currin's Ltd. and Hobby Junction, opened on the same day to officially open the new Mall shopping area.

David smiles as T.B. Rose, Jr. cuts the ribbon at the Rose's Grand opening of the mall shopping area.

By June 1973, South Hills Mall and Plaza, as well as the surrounding outparcels, housed 41 businesses including: the anchor stores—Roses and Winn Dixie, Radio Shack, Walker Shoes, The Hobby Shop, Hallmark Cards, Jordan's Jeans South, The Furniture Gallery, House of Carpet, Kerr Drugs, Heritage Jewelers, Recordillo, Steve's Hardware, Mark Anthony's Hairstyling, South Hills Barbershop, and Gino's Italian Restaurant.[54]

The year 1973 was also the year David, then 45 years old, ran for a seat on the Cary Town Council. He had his eyes set on being elected mayor by his fellow councilmen, should he win his race. He advocated for a conservative city government approach that would not overburden the city's taxpayers or property owners.[55] His supporters handed out two types of literature. One handout contained a photo of David, Marilyn, and their children and described how David's experience as a businessman and developer would benefit the town. The flier also stated his only promise to voters was to represent them the way he would want to be represented. The other handout had a copy of a $10 bill on one

---

[54] "South Hills Mall and Shopping Center," (advertisement), *The Cary News*, June 6, 1973, p. 9, col. 2.

[55] Martin Joins Council Race, *The Raleigh Times*, October, 1973.

side. Written on the opposite side were these words: "This is not real, but it could be if you vote for David Martin to help you save your tax dollars, Tuesday, November 6." According to David's eldest daughter, Donna, "Daddy's handout was what looked like a folded $10 bill; many people thought it was a bribe." David realized afterward that this second handout had been a mistake. He lost the election, and Fred G. Bond was re-elected mayor by his colleagues.

Having lost the town council election, David turned his attention back to his business endeavors. Less than a year later, between July and November of 1974, the mall was burglarized five times and vandalized at least once. David responded by posting signs that read: "$500 reward to anyone shooting a burglar on these premises, only $200 for apprehension." [56]

Area newspapers picked up the story of $500 reward for shooting a burglar at South Hills Malls, but David meant for the sign to be a deterrent.

---

[56] "At Cary shopping center, Open Season on Burglars," Raleigh Times, Nov. 13,1974.

South Hills merchants had noticed a significant increase in shoplifting, and David was trying his best to come up with a solution. Area newspapers picked up the story, and the signs became a local topic of conversation. The controversy then spread to the national news, and the noted broadcaster Paul Harvey even mentioned it in one of his radio programs.

The controversy over the signs lasted a week. Wake County Superior Court Judge James H. "Pou" Bailey weighed in and told *The News and Observer* that if someone was shot and killed because of the signs, the shooter would face a charge of murder and would probably be convicted. He also stated, "There is also a good chance the owner of the shopping center would be charged with accessory after the fact of murder, which carries a maximum penalty of life in prison." Additionally, Cary Police Chief J.W. Boles said he feared burglars who were aware of the signs would choose to arm themselves. However, the chief acknowledged he had checked with a lawyer and was informed the signs were legal.[57] David maintained he posted them as a preventative measure and cited his experience deterring burglaries at the mall's service station by posting a similar sign there.[58] Not one burglary occurred at the station in the 10-year period after the sign was posted. However, a short time after that interview, David took the signs down. In a subsequent interview with *The Cary News*, David explained that the hassle the situation caused and concerns the signs might lead to lower sales led him to take them down voluntarily. "Now I will let the police do what they ought to do," he said.[59]

---

[57] Judge Hits 'Bounty' Signs at Mall," *The News and Observer*, November 14, 1974, p. 49.

[58] "Martin Removes Bounty Signs," The Cary News, November 20, 1974, p. 19.

[59] "Martin Removes Bounty Signs," The Cary News, November 20, 1974, p. 19.

CHAPTER 19

Growing Up at the Mall

Fathers, do not exasperate your children; instead,
bring them up in the training and instruction
of the Lord. (Ephesians 6:4 NIV)

While David pursued various civic affairs and business opportunities in the early 1970s, his children were growing up, and the family dynamic was changing. In 1973, when he ran for the seat on the Cary Town Council, David, Jr. was 17, Donna 16, Dotty 14, Dale 12, Diane 10, and Debbie was 6. Most of their lives their mother had been a stay-at-home mom until that same year she decided to go back to work. She became the manager of the University Apartments leasing office, which was then located in the office building at 3700 Western Blvd. Debbie recalled: "She came to me when I was six and said, 'I'd like to go back to work, is that OK?' and it just tickled me that she would ask me. She ran the apartment office. I would go with her to work or she would pick me up after school. I'd go and I would answer the phone, in a child's voice, 'University Apartments.' It was wonderful to grow up in business."

Having a father whose business portfolio included a mall meant the Martin children also spent a lot of time there. Debbie and her siblings had free reign to explore the mall and to play games.

Diane (left) and Dale (right) grew up
at the mall and played games there.

They found a unique way to use the remaining folded "$10 bills" David had used to promote his candidacy during the election. Debbie recalled: "We would go into the Roses that used to be on the other side of the mall where the Tuesday Morning is now and take those "$10 bills." We would put them on the ground or on a spot where somebody could see them. We'd sit and watch people react when they thought they had found money. One lady bent down, looked around quickly and stuck it in her bra. We hid them all over the Roses store." Debbie added that she and Diane would go into the Kerr Drugs and throw the change they had been saving on the ground to count out the money they needed to buy candy. The manager, an older man, hated for them to do this. When he caught Debbie in the act, he sometimes hooked her with his cane and yelled at her.

Diane loved going to the mall with her family on Saturday nights to listen to the Revelators. "Russell was my favorite in that group" she said. "That was just a big thing, to go there and listen to the gospel music.

The Martin family loved listening to Gospel music at South Hills.

Then when I was a little bit older, Vicky's Calabash Seafood was at the mall, and we would go there on Friday nights. Back in the day, when Vicky's was at the mall, when we would go there we would see a lot of people from the community. The community was smaller, and everybody knew everybody. It was just a real family-oriented restaurant."

The mall was not only a fun place for the Martin children. They also learned life lessons there. On one occasion, Debbie grew thirsty and poured herself a soda from a vendor's dispenser despite the refreshment stand being closed for business. In her child's mind she thought it was okay to do it since her father owned the mall. When David found out she had taken the drink, he was very angry with her. David scolded her, then took her back to the stand when it reopened so she could apologize to the vendor for taking his merchandise. The incident marked the only time that David spoke to her in such a disgusted tone. All the Martin children also worked at the mall during their formative years. They either worked for some of the store owners, helped to manage the mall, or planned for civic events. Eventually, David, Jr. and Diane's husband, Will, all owned stores there, and even Donna and Dale took a turn at retail by opening "Small Blessings" children's boutique.

While David's children were learning life lessons and how to work at the mall, the general contracting portion of David's business was changing too. David had been given a lot of leeway concerning compliance with local building codes during his early projects. However, he was now facing increasing pressure to abide absolutely by the codes of the various municipalities in which he did business. So ingrained in his mind was the habit of avoiding waste at all costs and so pressing was the need for his business to avoid any unnecessary spending that David built houses and buildings with the materials he had on hand, at times not having the resources to comply with what the local building codes said.

Also, he lost his mall manager, Joyce Hawley, who was forced to resign her position after a serious automobile accident. It took two years for her to fully recover from her injuries. Although it seemed that she and David Martin had, out of necessity, gone their separate ways, their paths would cross again just a few years later.

CHAPTER 20

Reaping the Lord's Harvest

Let us not become weary in doing good, for at the proper time
we will reap harvest if we do not give up. (Galatians 6:9 NIV)

These difficulties did not keep David from continuing to share the Gospel with as many people as possible. Beginning in the late 1960s and continuing to the present, David expanded his efforts to spread the message of Christ by joining the Gideons, the international association of believers who provide Bibles to hospitals, hotels, prisons, universities, and other public institutions at no charge. They also personally share the Gospel worldwide with people from all walks of life.

David stayed true to his conviction that he should reach out to young people and regularly visited the Raleigh Military Entrance Processing Station (MEPS), as well as the Polk Youth Correctional Center, and the North Carolina Correctional Institution for Women, which were also in the city.

Donna Martin Evenson, who accompanied her father when he began going to the Raleigh MEPS, recalled how he interacted with the staff at the induction center: "At first the staff there said they would give out the Bibles he brought. Then he won over the people at the desk, and they would make an announcement for all inductees to report to a certain room. He'd deliver the Plan of Salvation—then ask how many people would like to accept Christ as their Savior. Sometimes he'd have a group of nearly 30 people pray to receive Christ."

David's passion and devotion for the lost gained the respect of many who heard him, and he often took other Gideons under his wing, teaching them how to reach out to the lost as well. Before his death in March 2016, Dr. Al Johnson, a Fuquay-Varina optometrist, credited David with teaching him how to share the Gospel message with a large audience when they witnessed together on one occasion at the Raleigh MEPS in the early 1970s. He recalled that David Spoke with conviction when he addressed the crowd, telling the recruits it was great to see them serving their nation, but they needed to know whether they were going to heaven or hell before they stepped into harm's way. Afterward, at David's invitation, 20 people accepted Christ. Dr. Johnson was excited about their response to the Gospel and awed by the fact that such a large portion—two-thirds—of the young men had responded to David's message. He told himself, "Man, oh man! I've been many places and I've never seen anything like this; man alive!" Soon after, Dr. Johnson was witnessing to new recruits on his own!

The two men would cross paths many times at the Raleigh MEPS and at Gideon state conventions. They also supported each other in the work of spreading the word of God wherever it was needed. Once, a snow storm was headed from the Fuquay-Varina area toward Raleigh. Dr. Johnson was scheduled to speak to the recruits at the MEPS station at 7 a.m. But the visibility was so low, he feared that he might wreck his car if he made the hour-long drive to Raleigh. He did not want the recruits to miss an opportunity to hear the Gospel and was at a loss about who he could ask to take his place. Then he thought of David, who lived much closer to the MEPS, and David agreed to substitute for him. "I didn't want to risk my life and get into a car wreck," Dr. Johnson said. "David didn't even hesitate. He said, 'I'll get there and get back before the snow gets too heavy.'"

In later years, the two also participated in Gideon mission trips when their chapters served in major population centers in the South. The cities they served included: Asheville, NC; Richmond, VA; Atlanta, GA; and Charleston, SC. While in those cities they passed out Bibles and witnessed to people in hospitals, motels, on the streets, or anywhere else they encountered them, and David was a shining example among his peers. "Wherever he went, he was a spokesman for God," Dr. Johnson said. "He also taught me about going out witnessing, and he made a great impact in my life."

Besides taking part in the Gideon's MEPS ministry, David was a well-known Christian speaker and was invited to speak at many churches throughout eastern North Carolina as well as in neighboring states—in Myrtle Beach, South Carolina, for example.

On one occasion, David was asked to be the keynote speaker for a revival at Piney Plains Christian Church, not far from South Hills Mall. Piney Plains was a small church with a membership that was not growing as it should. David told the pastor that if they were going to hold a revival, he wanted to go out the Saturday before the service to witness to the church's neighbors. When they discussed where they would go, the pastor said they would waste their time if they went to visit Connie Campbell, Jr., because he had no interest in coming to church. David told the pastor, "No, that's the first place we should go to." When David knocked on his door, Mr. Campbell's wife answered and told him her husband was in the shop behind their house. David recalled meeting Mr. Campbell: "He met me in the yard, and I said, 'Connie can I talk to you about the Lord?' And he said, 'Yes, but I don't make quick decisions.'"

David shared the Gospel and prayed with Connie Campbell, pictured above, and the next day he was baptized and made a commitment to follow God.

After talking some more, the two men got on their knees. They prayed to God about Mr. Campbell's decision to become a Christian. At the revival the following day, about 16 people came forward to be baptized. The tallest man in the group was Connie Campbell. Mr. Campbell maintained his devotion to God until his death in April 1972. Since then, the friendship between the Campbell and the Martin families has continued. Mr. Campbell's daughter-in-law, Bonnie, was a successful South Hills merchant for many years.

David would see more of the fruit of his labor several years later, in 1983. While worshipping at First Baptist Church in Cary, Mark Williams, a sailor, happened to see David entering the sanctuary. He walked up to David and introduced himself. In January of the prior year, Mark was in the meeting room when David addressed inductees at the Raleigh MEPS station. Mark said David caught his attention when he asked the audience if they had ever thought about death or dying. When Mark learned he could not get to heaven just by being a good 'ole Southern boy, he eagerly responded to David's call to repeat the Prayer of Salvation found at the back of every Gideon Bible, including the one David presented to him. He then signed his name in the back of that Bible as a declaration of his commitment to accept Jesus as his Lord and Savior. Back in Cary for his wedding, Mark related that when he saw David, he was very excited and said to his new wife: "There he is! There he is! That is the man that told me about Jesus."

"I thought I had lost that New Testament Bible until one day my three-year-old daughter came walking through the house with it in her hand." Mark continued, "She had marked it up with a crayon. Maybe she was trying to sign it too! I still have that Bible. I thank my Lord that Mr. Martin was faithful that Tuesday morning to share the good news with me that day. It changed my life!"

David's labor of love for the lost also bore fruit at Polk Youth Correctional Center where many young men with whom he shared the Gospel made a commitment to the Lord and were baptized. Such a large number of them were committing themselves to the Lord that David decided to build a baptismal pool at the prison. In a letter dated August 15, 1975, the Chaplain of Polk Youth Center expressed his great appreciation for David's work and thanked him for the new baptismal pool. While David shared the message of Christ with the young men, his interactions with them gave him a clear picture of the consequences faced by people who commit crimes while under the influence of drugs and alcohol. Becoming so affected by their troubles, David developed an even deeper conviction that he would never allow any of his businesses or properties to be used in any way to promote their use. For this reason, all of his commercial leases include covenants prohibiting the sale of alcohol. He continued to help prisoners whenever he could and to visit the Raleigh MEPS station until the late 1990s, when government rules changed to allow only the handing out of Bibles and would no longer allow for the personal witnessing that David had done so faithfully for many years.

But that did not stop David from witnessing in any other place that he could and to whomever he could. Throughout her high school years, Donna and her friends would regularly go to "Thursday night visitation," a house to house outreach effort, with David and other adults from First Baptist Church. On one occasion, Donna's friend asked that David visit her home so he could reach out to her father. The girls prayed together in the car while David led the friend's father to the Lord.

Not all of David's visits went so smoothly. On one occasion, in 1970 or 1971, David's nephew Steve Grissom accompanied him to a home in rural Apex, NC to share the Gospel with a young man about Steve's age whose father had contacted David. The father was deeply concerned about his teenage son, who, although he worked hard in the tobacco fields during the day, was hanging out with the wrong crowd at night. The father was afraid his son would soon be drawn into the drug culture, if he was not already. When David and Steve arrived at the home, the father told them, "I think he's out back." David replied, "Let's go look for him!" David and his nephew saw a shed and suspected the young man might be hiding behind it. They split up and approached it from the rear from opposite directions. It was very dark, so neither of them could see exactly where he was going. Suddenly, Steve felt something hit him hard in the back of the head. Steve felt a bit woozy but ran as fast as he could to get away from whomever or whatever had hit him! In the meantime, the young man, who was wielding what turned out to be a two-by-four, dropped his make-shift weapon and ran into the woods. David quickly followed Steve to ensure he was okay; he then suggested they try to re-approach the young man. But Steve would have nothing to do with this plan! He told David, "I'm not going to talk to him until he has better sense than to hit someone in the back of the head." In Steve's opinion, the prospect of that young man being receptive to the Gospel that night was remote! Steve remarked, "David was willing to go wherever he felt the Lord was leading him." However, at times like this Steve wished David had "thought a little before going!"

CHAPTER 21

Daddy Knows Best

He will yet fill your life with laughter and your lips with sounds of joy. (Job 8:21 NIV)

A father with five daughters is eventually going to have to meet the young men they date. Most likely he will interact with their boyfriends, too. David Martin was no different. Donna was the eldest daughter of his five girls.

Donna, during her junior year in high school.

In the mid-1970s, she was the first one out of the gate onto the dating scene. When she started dating, one of her cousins set her up with a young man who kissed her on the first date. She said his forward behavior deeply upset her. "I thought you ought to wait till the third date until you kissed someone." She waited until he came to her house again to tell him she had to stop dating him because he moved too fast. As she was relaying the news to him, a red sports car drove up. Basil, a young man she had met at the beach that past summer, hopped out of it. He had driven all the way from West Virginia to surprise her! When she saw Basil pull up to her parents' house, she ran out to meet him, leaving the "kissing bandit" on the porch. The rejected suitor left when he saw Basil. David, who had overheard her conversation with the "kissing bandit" and noticed Donna's reaction when Basil arrived, fell on the ground laughing. Her fling with Basil was short-lived, however, as Basil soon returned home. Not long after Basil left, Donna was the one who was let down. She dated a young man, Greg, who eventually broke up with her. One day she was alone in her room, missing her boyfriend, when David went in and sat down to talk with her. He did his best to console her over the break-up. It was a scene that would repeat itself many times during his daughters' teen years.

David was stricter with his three older children when they began dating than he was with his younger three. This was evident when his middle daughter, Dale, who knew more about gospel bands than secular ones, developed a love of going out dancing with her friends. David, ever the staunch Baptist, did not approve of this activity. When he learned one night of her plan to go out dancing at a local college hangout on Raleigh's Hillsborough Street, he decided to go find her. Dale and her friend evaded him that night by ducking down when he came looking for them! Her father was not against any of his daughters having an interest in young men or going on dates. He just wanted them to do so in a manner he felt was appropriate. In fact, he told his daughters, "Watch your figure, or the boys won't." Diane, who began dating a few years later, could not remember any specific rules they had to follow on dates. Debbie, his youngest, said, "He just wanted to know if the guys I dated were Christians. He would embarrass me when I was with my friends. He would say, 'And if you die, where are you going tonight?' They just knew to expect that they were going to have some kind of spiritual conversation with him when they came over."

CHAPTER 22

The Pan Incident

"Go," said Jesus. "Your faith has healed you." (Mark 10:52 NIV)

While David's forthright way of discussing eternal salvation with their friends sometimes embarrassed his daughters, at other times his faith and trust in God's healing power left the girls wide-eyed with wonder. One example is how David responded to injuries he received while on a pan, or earth-moving machine, in 1975. As he was operating the pan, the radiator overheated, causing the machine to lurch. David stopped the machine so he could diagnose the problem. After investigating the cause, he realized what the problem was and unscrewed the radiator cap to release the pressure. The liquid sprayed out scalding his shoulders, hands, arms, and private parts. He was left with third-degree burns and was in excruciating pain. He immediately rushed home, intending to take a cold shower when he arrived, but David, Jr. was taking a shower in the bathroom. To make matters worse, young David had locked the bathroom door and could not hear his father frantically banging on it. David, Sr., who could no longer stand the pain, broke the door down, hustled his son out of the shower, and jumped in. Debbie and Diane, who were at home at the time, were horrified at the sight of their father's hands. They were burnt, and the peeling skin made it appear that he was wearing a pair of gloves over them. Soon afterward, David left the house for the hospital to seek treatment. The doctors offered him painkillers, but he refused to take them or to be seen by a plastic surgeon. Instead, he told them, "No. I'm going to trust in the Lord to heal me." Then he left. Resting at home and recuperating from his injuries were the furthest things from David's mind. He was determined not to miss his usual Saturday night stint as emcee for the gospel singing at South Hills Mall! That night, David put a pair of feminine pads on his shoulders to protect them and, dressed in a bathrobe, black business socks, and sandals, he took the stage!

David was determined not to miss church the following morning either. He arrived at Sunday services and took his position as greeter at the church entrance. That day, a man named Jimmy Walker visited the church for the first time. He had recently moved to North Carolina to start a new job, but his wife, Virginia, and his children, David and Myra, had not yet joined him. The first person he saw at the church door was David, with his heavily bandaged hands raised high in the air! Jimmy was quite impressed by David's greeting, which, although it lacked a handshake, lacked nothing in friendliness and sincerity. He was amazed that someone in David's condition could even make it to church, much less carry on his normal duties there. Jimmy and his entire family later joined First Baptist in Cary and were members there for many years. Along the way, Myra Walker and David's daughter Diane became close friends, and that friendship has lasted until this day. Both women and their spouses attend Hope Community Church, another church with which the Martin family is closely associated. As for David's injuries, to the amazement of his family and friends and a true testimony to his faith, David has no visible scarring on his hands or shoulders from the accident!

CHAPTER 23

Change and Challenges

I have told you these things, so that in me you may have peace. In this world you will have trouble. But take heart! I have overcome the world." (John 16:33 NIV)

David, Jr. and Donna graduated from Cary High School in 1975. That fall, David, Jr. enrolled at Wingate College to begin taking core education classes. At the same time, Donna entered UNC-Chapel Hill and decided to double major in recreation administration and psychology. She graduated three years later.

*David, Jr. and Donna were members of
Cary High School's Class of 1975.*

David and Marilyn did not have long to bask in the success of having two children graduate from high school. Even with $500,000 from the 1973 sale of some of their properties to the DeAngelis brothers—the owners of Amedeo's restaurant—the Martins still had a cash flow problem. To make matters worse, David's business partner in a hotel venture in Durham, NC, pulled out of the project, leaving David with all the bills. David tried everything he knew to "stay afloat."

Winn-Dixie left South Hills, and 12 other tenants whose businesses depended on the customer traffic that the grocery store generated followed suit, not only leaving South Hills but defaulting on their debts. On June 27, 1975, South Hills Shopping Center, Inc. was forced to file for a Chapter 10 reorganization with the U.S. Federal Court, Eastern District of NC. In a Chapter 10 reorganization, as in its replacement, the Chapter 11 reorganization, the management of the entity the court was asked to help was displaced for a designated time. In the management's stead the court appointed a receiver or trustee to handle its duties and to oversee the reorganization or restructuring process. Attorneys J. Larkin Pahl, a bankruptcy expert, and Fred Smith, who later became a prominent businessman and politician, were appointed by the court as receivers. The court charged them with the responsibility of helping David get South Hills Shopping Center, Inc. back on solid footing again, so they could return it to him.

Neither Mr. Pahl nor Mr. Smith had any experience leasing commercial property or running a mall. They needed someone who could help them with these tasks and who could help them work with David. Some might call it fate, but David would see it as Divine Providence. Mr. Pahl called Joyce Hawley. He told her about the reorganization and their need for someone who could help them get the mall up and running again.

After Winn-Dixie and its 12 neighboring tenants left the shopping center, David started losing hundreds of thousands of dollars in revenue. By the time the newly-appointed receivers brought in Joyce to run the mall, rent from tenants had dwindled to $15,000-$18,000 per month. Many of the tenants she signed on had also left the mall. "Well, there were a few, maybe five or six tenants left that I knew, including Roses and Kerr Drugs and one or two more," she said.

Even with someone like Joyce Hawley at the helm, it was difficult for David, who had always had total control of his own assets, to conceive that someone else was running his business and had the authority to tell him how he should operate it. Marilyn was also under a tremendous amount of stress, especially after a deputy sheriff and other court officials came to their home to assess the value of their household goods in preparation for seizure. The stress was almost more than she could endure, but David said he continued to put his trust in the Lord. He slept well and appeared to be worry free.

On one occasion Wake County Sheriff Robert Pleasants and his deputies were ordered to come the following day to remove items from the Martins' home. Sheriff Pleasants was very uncomfortable with the idea of carrying out this order. His own family was deeply rooted in the Cary area, and he had known the Martins for years. The night before the scheduled seizure, he was plagued with terrible dreams about what he had been ordered to do. As a result, the next day Sheriff Pleasants asked the judge handling the matter to allow David more time to come up with the money to make at least a partial payment on some of his debt. The plea the sheriff made on David's behalf persuaded the judge to allow this time, thus sparing the entire Martin family the humiliation and trauma they would have experienced if the sheriff had taken their property.

While things looked bad for David on the home front, the receivers unwittingly did him a favor when they hired Joyce Hawley. Joyce sincerely wanted to save South Hills Mall and to restore it to the mall she had left several years before. She spearheaded the formation of the South Hills Merchants Association, which addressed concerns of the various tenants. She worked with the Association's members to beautify the mall building and grounds, and she raised rents to increase the mall's cash flow.

Joyce had been at the mall for nearly a year when she was asked to meet with the court-appointed receivers. At that meeting, she suggested that South Hills become a discount mall, a concept that was becoming popular in the 1970s. But Smith and Pahl nixed that idea. Joyce worked an additional week, then she resigned. Mr. Pahl tried to convince her to stay, but she stood by her earlier position and turned him down. Joyce had the last laugh when David renamed the mall South Hills Outlet Mall in the summer of 1980. The mall operated under this name until 1991.

Despite the difficulties she encountered during the mall's reorganization, Joyce maintained everyone always knew David's heart was good. "He's only one of two people that I know that is so tough that you can hold their head down in a bucket of water for 15 minutes, let them up and they would come up and say, 'Boy didn't that feel good!' I will tell you, I think David is a good man, as far as being who he is in all circumstances. As my ex-father-in-law would say, 'He's a curious wrinkle.'"

Amid the chaos the Chapter 10 reorganization caused David and his family, Donna met Eric Evenson while she was at UNC-Chapel Hill, and they began dating in December of 1975. She introduced him to her parents over her birthday dinner the next month. The plan was for Eric to meet Donna's entire family at the Carolina Inn at 6 p.m. The young couple arrived on time and waited for her parents to show up. They waited until 8 p.m., when the inn's restaurant closed. Cell phones were not in use yet, so they could not call Donna's parents to find out what had happened. They continued to wait. Finally, her family arrived, and fortunately they found another restaurant that was open! During the meal Diane and Dale argued over whose steak was the rarest. One of Donna's sisters tripped Eric every time he got up to go to the salad bar. But Eric admired her Dad and thought he could do no wrong. To be suddenly thrust into this large "All-American" family was quite an experience for Eric, who came from a small family of Scandinavian descent.

Eric and Donna continued to date for a few years and, though David trusted them, he admonished the young couple to "abstain from the appearance of evil." "We had to have a chaperone," Donna explained, which in most cases was one of her siblings. Debbie was the chaperone when Donna and Eric took a weekend trip to the beach and stayed at his grandfather's trailer. Unfortunately, Debbie stayed out in the sun too long the day they arrived and became ill. The next day, instead of taking her back home, they went to church because David insisted his family never miss a service, and Donna was afraid he would be upset if they did not go. Debbie did not feel well enough to attend, so Eric and Donna left her resting in the car while they attended the worship service.

When Eric visited Donna at her parents' home, no chaperone was required, but David did find a way to check on them. During one visit, Eric and Donna were sitting in the den when a noise startled them. They saw David and one of her young sisters crawling across the floor of the dining room and peeking through the door at them. Apparently, David was teaching his children to be spies!

In April 1976, while South Hills was still under the reorganization, things went from bad to worse. David received a notice from the Wake County Superior Court that the NC Board of Transportation intended to exercise its right of eminent domain and take 44 acres of his property along Buck Jones Road to complete the construction of Interstate 40 and its interchange with U.S. Highway #1. David was devastated. The taking of his land meant the death of his dream of building the first large-scale regional mall in the area, once he regained control of his company. Not legally in control of South Hills, he was in no position to fight the seizure. In December of the same year, the state paid the receivers approximately $10,000 an acre for 44 acres—$440,000 for the land David and Marilyn had worked so hard to acquire. The money from the sale of the land immediately went to repay debts associated with the reorganization.

CHAPTER 24

The Return of the Mall

*But thanks be to God! He gives us the victory through
our Lord Jesus Christ. (1 Corinthians 15:57 NIV)*

Time moves on, and the mid-to-late 1970s were a busy time for David
and Marilyn. Dotty graduated from Cary High School in 1977.

Dotty in her 1977 Cary High School graduation cap and gown.

Donna continued to date Eric, who graduated from UNC with a
Bachelor of Arts degree (B.A.) in History and Politics the same year. He
then enrolled in law school at Wake Forest University in Winston-Salem,
NC. Donna graduated from UNC in 1978 with a B.A. in Recreation
Administration and Psychology.

Though David was busy, he still managed to find ways to encourage his children still living at home. Sometimes these efforts almost backfired on him. Both Dale and Diane had reached the age at which they could drive. David went home one day and told them, "I bought you each a new car!" Dale said he was very excited and took them for a ride in the family car to see the vehicles he had picked out for them. Along the way, they peppered him with questions about the cars' make and model. It turned out they were identical older, light-blue Dodge Dart Swinger models. "They were the ugliest cars I've ever laid my eyes on," Dale said. They turned out, however, to be very well-made. While Dale was driving back with a friend to UNC-Wilmington after a weekend visit with her parents, a deer ran right into her car. The poor animal did not leave as much as a dent on the vehicle!

In the meantime, Donna and Eric's love for each other had grown. During a visit to the Martins' home, a nervous Eric met with David in his office to ask for his sweetheart's hand in marriage. Even on a shoestring budget, love doesn't wait. Eric and Donna were married at First Baptist Church of Cary, on June 25, 1978.

Eric and Donna on the day of their wedding, in June 1978.

Times were still tough for the Martins financially so Grandmother Lillie Broadwell made all the bridesmaids dresses. Donna's wedding dress was purchased for $150. The whole family worked together, under David and Marilyn's direction, to make mints for the wedding reception. Debbie remembered tray after tray of the delicious smelling and tasting mints laying on the kitchen table and countertops. Donna made her own wedding cake.

The newlyweds moved to Winston-Salem, NC, so Eric could complete his last two years of law school at Wake Forest University. During the week Donna stayed in Cary with her parents while she commuted to Southeastern Seminary in Wake Forest, NC, where she was enrolled in the master's degree program in religious education. On weekends she drove home to Winston-Salem to be with Eric. Donna completed her degree in 1980, and Eric graduated from law school shortly thereafter. They lived in Greensboro for a few months, but later moved to Durham where they lived while Eric served as an assistant district attorney for Durham County. In 1990, Eric became an Assistant U.S. Attorney for the Eastern District of NC. He was chief of the district's organized crime and drug enforcement task force and worked hard to get drug dealers out of towns in Eastern North Carolina. He and David used to say that Eric would arrest and send criminals to prison so David could go in and lead them to the Lord! When Eric retired from the federal government, in 2013, he had also worked in the district's anti-terrorism unit for several years.

To the Martins' immense relief, on January 20, 1979, the Wake County Superior Court returned control of South Hills Shopping Center, Inc. to David. In charge of its operations again, he focused on improving the appearance of the mall and righting what he believed to be a wrong. He filed a lawsuit disputing the fairness of the price the state paid for the 44 acres of land taken from him. Because this land was located along the route of the future Interstate 40 and the interchange with U.S. Highway 1 & 64, traffic patterns would have brought thousands of people each day to his planned regional mall. Friends from First Baptist Church collected money to help him hire a lawyer, and in May 1979 the matter came up before the Wake County Superior Court. One of the developers of Cary Village Mall, later known as Cary Towne Center, testified before the jury that he would not have been able to build his mall, which had opened in February 1979, if David had not lost his land to the state. The jury agreed with David and awarded him $1,188,740, nearly three times the amount the state originally paid for the land, plus interest. This amount represented what was at that time the largest land condemnation award ever received by anyone from the State of North Carolina.

David was grateful to God for bringing him through the greatest trial of his business career. In response to what the Lord had done for him, he insisted that all people and businesses who had loaned money to him be repaid in full, even though the court did not require him to do so. David's top priority was paying $86,394 in back taxes and interest to the Town of Cary, and $147,055 to Wake County. One company he especially wanted to repay was Burke Brothers Hardware. The Burkes had stood by him during some of his toughest times. Martin Properties remains one of the store's most loyal customers. As he had done before, David used any money left over from repaying his debts to make improvements at South Hills.

Incidentally, some people in the business community thought that when the 325,000-square-foot Cary Village Mall opened it would drive South Hills Mall out of business. However, David expressed the opposite opinion, saying he thought Cary Village would help South Hills. He explained why in an interview with the *Cary News* in 1989: "I knew that size center would have to draw a lot of people to this area. Our business, our volume went up the week we opened. We benefited." David has also always maintained the reason other malls or shopping centers have not hurt South Hills is because he offers lower rent to his tenants, and he refused to sell out. "Every time you sell out to a higher value, people will have to get more rent. I'm a local boy; I grew up here. I don't have anything for sale, especially to people who are not in the local area. They would just be in it for the bottom line. I've got a country boy philosophy: Pigs get fat and hogs get slaughtered. And I am not hoggish about my rent. I look after my tenants." [60]

Winning the large land condemnation award from the state coupled with the increasing foot traffic and revenue at the mall were very good reasons to celebrate. However, in June 1979, David and Marilyn had another very special reason to celebrate—their 25th wedding anniversary! David wanted to commemorate the day in some way, but he had always been a no-frills kind of guy. In fact, though he loaned Marilyn's family members money to buy new cars, he never bought a new car for himself.

---

[60] James Hyatt, "South Hills Mall Owner Expects to Benefit from Crossroads Mall," *The Cary News*, January 4, 1989.

Instead, his car has always been Marilyn's "hand-me-down" car after she purchased a new one. However, with his daughter Donna's encouragement, as an anniversary gift David purchased a 1-carat diamond wedding ring for Marilyn from a local pawn shop. That diamond ring remains not only a monument to the length of their marriage but is also a symbol of the ups and downs they have shared and their unwavering love for each other.

Having weathered the storm of reorganization, David and Marilyn watched and, in most cases, celebrated as their children's lives rapidly changed. In 1980, Dale graduated from high school and went on to major in criminal justice at UNC-Wilmington. Dotty graduated from UNC-Chapel Hill with a Bachelor of Science degree in Nursing the following year. While attending the university, she met Jeffrey "Jeff" Reintgen, a wrestler on an athletic scholarship. One thing that impressed Dotty about Jeff was his involvement in Bible study. Inevitably, the two began dating. She introduced him to her parents when they met for dinner at a pizza restaurant in Cary. David invited Jeff to accompany him on one of the Gideon outreach visits to Polk Youth Center the next day. He also put Jeff up in a motel overnight so he would not have to drive home.

On June 20, 1981, Dotty Jo and Jeff were married at First Baptist Church in Cary. He decided to pursue a calling to the ministry and attended Rhema Bible Training Academy in Broken Arrow, OK, for two years.

Jeff and Dotty were married at
First Baptist Church of Cary, in June 1981.

Dotty said her father was always very supportive of Jeff's call to the ministry. In fact, she added, her father paid a year's tuition for her to attend the same school and therefore become better equipped for her role as a pastor's wife. Dotty worked as a nurse in Tulsa during the year both she and Jeff attended Bible college. Afterward, the couple moved to Latrobe, PA, where they pastored the Latrobe Christian Center, a full gospel church, for eight years. Dotty also continued her nursing career in Greensburg, PA., working in both the dialysis unit and on the medical floor of the local hospital.

While Jeff and Dotty were serving in Latrobe, the church leadership decided to buy land in order to construct a new building to meet the congregation's needs. Dotty said her dad flew to Latrobe to look at the property and offer his advice about how the church should proceed. While attending the Sunday service, David walked around and wrote down the names and contact information for each person he met, even though his stay would be short. In later conversations with Jeff and Dotty, David made it a point to inquire by name about the welfare of some of the people he had met.

CHAPTER 25

A Baby No More

Be kind and compassionate to one another, forgiving each other, just as in Christ God forgave you. (Ephesians 4:32 NIV)

In August 1982, John Eric Evenson, III, Eric and Donna's first child, was born. David and Marilyn became youthful and energetic grandparents at the ages of 54 and 49, respectively.

*John Eric Evenson, III, the Martin's first grandchild,
was born in August 1982.*

The 1980s would bring more grandchildren into David and Marilyn's lives, but they weren't empty nesters until later in the decade. Their youngest daughter, Debbie, was only 15 when John was born.

Amid the ongoing hustle and bustle of David's life, his son an daughters' lives continued to flourish. After graduating from high school in 1982, Diane enrolled at Campbell University in the small Harnett County town of Buies Creek, NC, where she majored in elementary education. While there she met William "Will" Stephenson, Jr., and they began dating. Will recalled that he met David on a Friday afternoon, in August 1983, when he and Diane returned home for a weekend visit. At the time, David was at the controls of his pan, or earth moving machine, grading the parking lot of the future Burlington Coat Factory at South Hills Mall. Later, the three walked over to the plaza for further conversation.

Debbie was still at home when her sisters started college. During this time, she began to actively pursue her own interests and reveal her unique personality. When Debbie was 12 years old, her parents sent her for a year of lessons at the local John Robert Powers Modeling School. There she learned how to coordinate the fashion shows that were being held at the mall. "I would pick about 25 people of all different shapes and sizes—men, women, and children," she said. "I would teach them how to walk. I also would work with each of the stores to find the clothing they wanted represented." Not only did Debbie serve as the shows' emcee, but she also wrote her own scripts, including descriptions of the clothing worn by each model. In addition, she coordinated the music for each show.

Debbie was not spoiled. None of the Martin children were. Though their family business brought in a significant amount of money, their parents lived frugally. She and her siblings each worked in some part of the business at one time or another. She recalled that during the period when her father's company went through reorganization and he nearly lost everything, he paid her a quarter an hour to paint window sills at the plaza. When she complained about the heat, he told her, "Keep working! Keep working!" Even though at the time it was hard to keep going, later in life, when she had a job working 60-plus hours per week, she came to appreciate her father's lessons in perseverance. In her mind she could still hear his voice saying, "Keep working! Keep working!" and that voice helped her to push through her fatigue.

Debbie sometimes made things interesting for her parents. On one occasion, she was at her friend Elizabeth's home. They were waiting for a third friend, Lisa, to drop by. When Lisa did not show up on time,

Debbie and Elizabeth called her house, but the phone was busy. It just so happened that Elizabeth's cousin, who was a year older than her, and one of her friends were also visiting Elizabeth's place that day. This friend had a new car, and Elizabeth and Debbie asked if she could drive them to Lisa's house. The younger girls were curious as to why Lisa's phone line was constantly busy.

*Debbie, 15, learned some valuable
lessons from the experience.*

Unfortunately, Elizabeth's friend said no; she could not do it. Not one to give up easily, Debbie volunteered to drive to Lisa's house. When Elizabeth heard that she perked up. She knew where her sister kept the keys to her old-beat-up station wagon. She gave them to Debbie, who drove toward Lisa's house. "My mind was just not thinking," Debbie said. "You know that age when you're not developed yet. I got about a half mile down the road when my mind caught up. I thought, 'What the heck are you doing?'" Though her father had let her steer his car when she was younger, he had never taught her how to drive. When she realized the position she had put herself in, she started getting jittery. Instead of stopping the car when she made it to Lisa's house, she drove past the house. She circled the cul-de-sac to see if the light in Lisa's room was on and then excitedly told Elizabeth they needed to head back to her home. To drive back to Elizabeth's home, they had to go down a small hill. Just as they started to head down the hill, the station wagon lost power, causing Debbie to lose the brakes. As the car coasted down the hill, she quickly assessed her options. Debbie concluded that if she drove straight, the road would end, and she would hit a grove of trees. If she turned to the left, she would hit some houses. If she turned to the right; she would ram into Elizabeth's apartment complex. She chose to take the right turn. By this time Elizabeth's cousin and the cousin's friend had gone to look for them. The friend parked her car on the side of the street at a stop sign and waited to see if Debbie would drive by. She did not have to wait long! Debbie's right turn caused her to careen into the parked car. The resulting crash totaled the friend's car and a nearby fire hydrant.

After the police arrived, they called David to tell him that Debbie had wrecked the car. At first, he refused to believe it because Debbie did not have a license. After he learned what happened, he realized, yes, it was her indeed! Needless to say, David and Marilyn grounded her. They also told her she would have to get a job so she could pay for damages to both cars. "My friends took up a collection, and I had to stay home on New Year's Day, which was the worst, because I'm a very social person," Debbie said. About a week went by, when on a Sunday afternoon, David said he wanted to take Debbie for a ride. She recalled what happened on their outing: "We got in the car, and he drove to my friend Elizabeth's house. He pulled up and said, 'Come here. I want to show you something.' I got out of the car, and there was the station wagon. The front of it looked like a Cadillac. He had made it look better than it did before. While I was admiring it, he said, 'This one is on me.' I was still trying to find a job to pay for the damages I caused, and I asked him what he was talking about. He said he had a confession to make, and I asked. 'What?' Then he smiled and said, 'I had my first accident before I had my license too!' I said, 'Dad! Why didn't you tell me that?' He told me, 'I had to let you suffer for a little while.' It was a powerful lesson. I learned a lot from that experience. Later, I told all my nephews, 'Don't you drive without a license!'"

The 1980s found David again totally immersed in his work at the mall. In 1983, Ray Cooke introduced him to William Horton. William, or "Horton" as he became affectionately known, had graduated from Cary High School the same year as David Jr. and Donna. He was the great nephew of Roxy Brewer, previously mentioned as one of David's dry-cleaning customers in the Asbury community back in the 1950s. Ray knew Horton from Athens Drive Baptist Church, where he was a member and where Horton worked as a custodian. Ray knew Horton needed more work and that David needed help at South Hills, so he made sure the two met. Mr. Horton continues to work for Mr. Martin as his main janitorial contractor. He also manages security for the shopping center.

David has always tried to help his employees whenever he can. Years later, when Horton needed a loan to buy a house, David lent him the money, enabling him and his wife, Edna, to have a place to live when they retire. Horton added that David is great to work for, and he could not have asked for a better boss.

While David was managing his work and family matters his mother, Euva Martin, who had been his faithful rock throughout his life, died in 1983 at the age of 88. She was short in stature and had been sickly most of her life.

Euva is pictured with six of her seven children, in April 1981, at a family gathering. (Top Row) L to R. Billy Martin, David J. Martin, Sr., George O'Briant. (Second Row) Martha Martin Grissom, Euva O'Briant Martin, Mary Blanch O'Briant Coston, and Euva Martin Freeze.

However, her example of deep Christian faith and dogged perseverance during the toughest of situations, especially during the Depression and World War II years, made her a giant in David's eyes and gave him a strong foundation from which he would face and survive the many storms of life yet to come.

CHAPTER 26

David Overcomes

Not only so, but we also glory in our sufferings, because we know that suffering produces perseverance; perseverance, character; and character, hope. And hope does not put us to shame, because God's love has been poured out into our hearts through the Holy Spirit, who has been given to us. (Romans 5:3-5 NIV)

One might say that in 1984, when David completed construction of the 100,000-square foot north end of South Hills Mall, he had weathered the storm and rebuilt his business. This project marked the end of the original construction of the mall, except for some outlying buildings constructed later. The completed South Hills was not the regional shopping center David had originally envisioned, and he had come close to losing it. Yet despite all the obstacles he had faced, he had built something of which he could not only be proud but that he could use as a tool to serve the community.

Bonnie Campbell, Connie Campbell's daughter-in-law and a long-time South Hills merchant, fondly remembered life at South Hills Mall during the 1980s and 1990s. "I helped with the mall promotions. We were all encouraged to get along. It was like a family. I don't think it would have been the same anywhere else." Bonnie started out working in the mall for a women's store and later became the manager for Country Sonshine. After managing the store for seven years, she bought the store, becoming its sole proprietor. Building on the success of the previous owner, Bonnie sold collectibles, candles, and other gift items, as well as furniture and other household goods.

She added that a portion of the Merchants Association dues were used to pay for television advertising. South Hills became in trade lingo, a "destination mall." Customers patronized these merchants not because of their size but because of the specialty items they offered. Merchants Association members worked together to ensure that mall facilities were kept in good repair and maintained their attractive appearance. Bonnie remembered that one year, David's daughter Dale worked with the merchants to choose different colors for each of their store fronts and have them painted to look like a row of houses! Other signature promotional events Dale started while working at South Hills were monthly Senior Citizens' Days and the "Live Reindeer Exhibit," which became an exclusive Christmas display at South Hills that lasted many years, bringing in many large crowds of customers until the NC Wildlife Commission ended the transportation of herd animals into the state due to health concerns.

Even though Bonnie decided to close her business in 2003, she has remained a loyal friend and supporter of South Hills and returns every Christmas to share her considerable decorating talents. In 2015, she was given permission by mall management to erect a life-size Nativity scene at the mall's busiest entrance. This display was repeated for Christmas 2016 and 2017, and there are no plans to discontinue it. Customers appreciate this expression of the true meaning of Christmas and the lack of the crass commercialism often found at other shopping venues.

One additional thing Bonnie appreciated about David was the time he took to speak to her grandson, Campbell Judy, about God. Campbell literally grew up at the mall. His grandmother often kept him beside her in his playpen there while she worked. When Campbell was five or six years old, he began to ask questions and show an interest in learning about God. When David heard about Campbell's curiosity, he began setting aside some time every Monday to talk to the young boy in his office. The two of them discussed what Campbell was learning in his Sunday School classes. Eventually, David gave every one of Bonnie's grandchildren a Gideon Bible.

David and Marilyn were not only enjoying how well things were going at the mall in 1984, but also rejoiced at other happy occasions. Dale graduated with her B.A. in Criminal Justice from UNC-Wilmington. She was hired at the Wake County Juvenile Treatment Center, where she worked for two years.

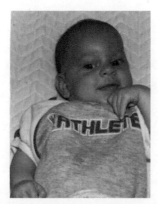

Mathew "Matt" David Reintgen, the Martins'
second grandson, was born in June 1984.

In June, their family expanded again when their daughter, Dotty Martin Reintgen, gave birth to her first child and David and Marilyn's second grandson, Mathew "Matt" David Reintgen.

CHAPTER 27

A Heart Attack Scare

The Lord sustains them on their sickbed and restores
them from their bed of illness. (Psalm 41:3 NIV)

Unfortunately, 1984 ended with David having a heart attack scare. At about 5:30 p.m. on December 17, 1984, while working on land he owned at 821 Buck Jones Rd, David started having excruciating chest pains and experiencing some shortness of breath. He decided to call it a day and drive home, which at the time was across the street from the mall. When he arrived, he sat down in front of an open window so he could get some fresh air while he read the newspaper and Marilyn cooked dinner. Never one to complain when he felt ill, he said nothing to his wife about the intense pain he felt. As he was reading, he came across the obituary section and learned that one of his friends had died. The visitation was scheduled that night. He asked his wife if she would drive him to the Brown-Wynne Funeral Home on Saint Mary's Street in Raleigh, but Marilyn said no; she had an oven full of cookies she was baking for Christmas. So, David drove himself!

After David left, Marilyn thought it peculiar that he would ask her to drive him, since he always drove himself wherever he needed to go. When he came home, she asked him the reason for his request. He then described the chest pains he had been experiencing. Alarmed, she told him he ought to seek medical help immediately, but he refused to do so.

The next day he got up as usual and went to work. Around 3 p.m. he drove back home to get something. When he arrived, his daughter Donna, pregnant at the time, was visiting her mother. Frantic with concern, she pleaded with him to go to his doctor's office to have his heart checked out. Donna recalled part of their conversation: "I was crying, and I said, 'If you don't go you might not be able to see my baby.'" He finally agreed to see the doctor. After what seemed like an eternity, Donna drove him in her own car to Dr. Fred Oliver's office. Upon their arrival around 5:30 p.m., Dr. Oliver and two other physicians examined David. They concluded he was on the verge of having a heart attack. They advised Donna to drive him immediately to Rex Hospital! He refused to go, but Donna told him she would not take him anywhere else. He threatened to walk home, so she tearfully told him that if he loved his family, he would go to the hospital as the doctors advised. David finally agreed to go to the hospital, but first he insisted on going home to take a shower.

> **"I don't know what the future holds, but I do know WHO holds the future."**
> **– David J. Martin**
> **One of David J. Martin, Sr.'s.**
> **favorite quotes**

When he arrived at the hospital David at first refused to be admitted, but his doctor insisted he stay for observation. He also ordered that David be placed on several medications to help prevent a heart attack and scheduled him for surgery. David promised the Lord then and there that if he could be healed and spared the upcoming procedure, he would devote the rest of his life to serving Him and bringing as many people as possible to know Him. David was hospitalized for about three days, but he was far from idle. He witnessed to people and passed out Gideon Bibles, sharing his faith with fellow patients, staff, and anyone else he encountered. In fact, two of his nurses accepted Christ after David shared the Plan of Salvation with them. David was discharged at 1:30 pm on December 20 and, in his words, "went back to work planting trees at South Hills Mall." He recalled, "I finally went home after dark, praising the Lord!" In the 33 years since this episode, David has never stopped giving God the glory for his recovery. Not long after this experience, David had a special dream. He related: "One night I had a dream of a large group of people and their pastor, none of whom I recognized. But the next day I opened a checking account, which I called South Hills Baptist Church. I set aside one and a half acres for the church building. I thought this parcel size would be adequate since I planned to permit parking on the surrounding land which our family owned. Later the Lord led me to realize that I was thinking too small. So, I set aside fourteen acres for a mega-church."

CHAPTER 28

Spreading Their Wings

And we know that for those who love God all things work together for good, for those who are called according to his purpose. (Romans 8:28 NIV)

While the other Martin children's lives were progressing, Debbie's path for the next several years began to take shape when she graduated high school in 1985.

Debbie graduated from Cary High School in 1985.

She enrolled at UNC-Wilmington, and majored in English, but she was not very focused on her studies. She had already worked in the movie industry for a year during high school at the now defunct De Laurentiis

Group Studios in Wilmington, N.C. While in college she was involved in the production of several movies, including *Crimes of the Heart* and *King Kong Lives*. The experience captured her imagination, leading her to conclude that she wanted a career in the movie industry. "All my friends were from Rome and L.A.," Debbie said. "I started hanging out with an older crowd. I just thought I knew better than anyone else at school. I was just arrogant. I loved film and being in that world. I'd go back to school only to be bored out of my mind." Eventually, after two-and-a-half years, Debbie dropped out of college

While Debbie was attending UNC-Wilmington, Diane completed her degree in elementary education, and graduated from Campbell University in 1986. Her boyfriend, Will, who attended the university for a year, decided to leave Campbell. He had majored in business administration and decided to pursue a business career in the "real world." He became part owner of Stereo Trends, a car stereo business which operated at the South Hills Plaza for 18 years. After Will and his partner decided to close the business, Will returned to school, this time at Wake Technical Community College. He earned both Type I and Type II Heating and Air Certifications and became a certified pool operator. Since 2003, Will has worked at the Martin Properties Residential Leasing Office, overseeing maintenance operations.

After he and Diane knew they wanted to marry, an extremely shy Will was too reticent to ask David for her hand in marriage. "It didn't matter, I was the fifth child," she said. While he did not ask for her hand in marriage, the two did play a practical joke that did not bother David and Marilyn much but thoroughly rattled Will's parents. "I sent them a letter through the mail. I told them that by the time they got it we were going to already be married in Florida," Diane said. "Will's parents called my parents all in a frazzle thinking we had eloped! Mom and Dad were just so calm about it." Jokes aside, Will and Diane tied the knot in June 1986 at First Baptist Church in Cary, in a lovely ceremony on the first day of summer.

Before they were married in June of 1986, Diane and Will played a joke on her parents and said they were eloping to Florida! (Top Row L to R) David, Sr, Diane, Will and Marilyn. Donna, John, and Dale. (Fourth Row) Debbie and David. Jr., Dotty and Matt.

At the beginning of their courtship, neither Diane nor Will realized that their fathers had already met. Will's father, William Stephenson, Sr., was a Raleigh police officer back in the 1960s when David was building University Apartments. A city road crew was doing some work in front of the property when a dispute arose over the right of way. David, already frustrated by regulatory roadblocks being put in his way by city officials, pulled out his shotgun to halt the crew's progress. When the police responded, it was Will's father who took charge and helped de-escalate the situation. "Who would have ever thought I would marry the son of the man who calmed my Dad down?" Diane mused.

While happy occasions came and went, there were times when the needs of the Martin family business demanded that David's children set aside their individual goals and devote their time to maintaining the enterprise. In 1986, David realized he needed help with South Hills Mall. He asked his daughter Dale to leave her job with Wake County and become the mall manager.

CHAPTER 29

Giving Back

Whoever is kind to the poor lends to the Lord, and He will reward them for what they have done. (Proverbs 19:17 NIV)

Though David was a busy man, he took every opportunity to help people who were willing to help themselves. An opportunity to help such a family presented itself in early February 1987. He was in his office at South Hills Mall when Casey Potter, a 27-year-old man from Kentucky, asked to speak to him. Casey told David he had decided to accept Jesus Christ as Lord and Savior after a visiting minister shared the Gospel with him during his incarceration at the Avery County Jail in Newland, NC. Casey explained that he had been sentenced to 14 years in prison for the 1984 robbery of handguns and rifles from a weapons collector. However, Casey had totally turned his life around as evidenced by his behavior during his trial and later while in prison. He became a model inmate and earned the right to work at the Governor's Mansion in Raleigh, serving as an assistant to Governor Jim Martin. Thanks to Governor Martin, Casey's 14-year sentence was commuted to time served—three years instead of the standard seven required by the law. Despite all the progress Casey had made while incarcerated, he realized he would need additional help once he was released. One day, Casey shared his concerns with a fellow inmate: He told the man his parents had put their lives in Kentucky on hold and moved to North Carolina to support him as he adjusted to life outside of prison. They had not found a place to live after he was released. They also had no jobs and no idea how they would get work. The inmate told Casey that he knew David Martin, the owner of South Hills Mall, and suggested that Casey make an appointment to see David, who might be willing to assist him. When David heard Casey's story he was moved to help him and his parents. What especially impressed David was the fact that Casey had ministered to other inmates during his incarceration.

He allowed the Potters to live in one of his duplex apartments in Triangle Forest, even though Casey had yet to begin his new job at a land survey company and despite his parents not having jobs. But David did not stop there.

"You can't out give God."
– One of David J. Martin. Sr.'s.
Favorite quotes

Casey recounted other things David did for him and his family. "Within a couple of hours, he pulled his vehicle in the driveway of the apartment he had provided us and asked us, 'Well what are you going to do for furniture? You're going to need furniture.' We said, 'Well, we haven't gotten that far yet,'" Casey recalled. 'We don't know what we are going to do,' and he told us to come back to his office. He made some phone calls, wrote down a lady's contact information on a piece of paper, and told us to go there so she could provide us with some furniture. I said, 'Mr. Martin, I really appreciate this, but we're not going to be able to buy any furniture until we work out a couple of paychecks.' He said, 'Son you don't need to take money down there with you. You just need to do what I am telling you and go down there. I'm taking care of all of that. These people are expecting you to come.' We went down there and the lady told us to pick out whatever we needed. We picked out a few pieces of furniture and she said, 'David told me you needed a whole house of furniture.' I said, 'Well we do, but we don't have any way to haul it. We're just trying to figure out how we are going to get this bed there along with these few pieces of furniture hauled out of here.' The lady said, 'Oh, you don't understand. We have a moving truck. We'll haul it and set it down. David arranged for that too. You just have to pick out what you want.' I just couldn't believe that all this was happening. I just couldn't believe anyone would help a stranger like he was doing. But he did. They came and delivered the furniture."

About a week later, David came by to see how the Potters were doing. When he learned they still had not found a church, he invited them to his own church, First Baptist in Cary. David also helped Casey's parents get jobs by calling some of his friends and personally vouching for them. He told Mrs. Potter to go to see Lamar Lloyd, the owner of The Little Red School House Daycare Center. She was hired on the spot. He then helped Mr. Potter, an auto mechanic, get a job at Crawford's Automotive Service in Holly Springs. "When the three of us got a couple of paychecks, we went to David's office and paid our rent that we owed him," Casey said. "We were not just going to stay there without paying anything."

He added that while David accepted the rent money they gave him, he set the rate below the rate he normally charged. After about six months, Casey completed his parole. His parents decided to leave their jobs and return home to Kentucky. When they left, Casey told David he no longer needed an apartment as large as the one he had shared with his parents and planned to move. David was not through helping him, though. He asked Casey to wait a minute while he called a friend. David persuaded her to rent an apartment to Casey at well below the market rate too.

Today, Casey Potter is an ordained minister and serves as the outreach director at Faith Christian Ministries in Sanford, NC. He said the reason his parents were able help him make the transition from prison to society was because David, "the man of God," was willing to help him after the manner of the Good Samaritan. As the Good Samaritan spared no trouble or expense to help the wounded traveler, so David stopped at nothing to help the Potter family in their time of need.

"He is what Christ was describing when he said, 'Do unto others as you would have them do unto you. Don't worry about the return because I will give you the return.' And that is the attitude that David has set forth to me," Mr. Potter said. "Every time I have been around him, every time I have had a conversation with him, he's not doing things because he is trying to get people to give him something. He's just trying to do what a good man of God ought to do, and that's what I've been trying to do these 30 years since I met him."

CHAPTER 30

Wedding Bells for Dale

*And now these three remain: faith, hope and love. But
the greatest of these is love. (I Corinthians 13:13 NIV)*

After graduating from college, Diane worked for a while as a part-time
teacher's aide at Underwood Gifted and Talented Magnet School in Raleigh.
Her supervising teacher, Mary Dascombe, had a son named Robert or "Bob."
He was single, and Diane's sister Dale was single. Diane and Mrs. Dascombe
collaborated and presented the idea to the two of them that they should
go out on a blind date. At the time, Bob had recently graduated from St.
Andrews Presbyterian College (now St. Andrews University) in Laurinburg,
NC. with a B.A. in Politics and a minor in Business Administration. His first
professional job in corporate America was as a claims adjuster for Nationwide
Insurance at the company's Fayetteville, N.C., office. Bob and Dale agreed
to meet for dinner at the Rock-Ola Café at Mission Valley Shopping Center
in Raleigh, about an hour's drive from Fayetteville. The two really did not
feel like going on a date that night. Bob was exhausted after having driven
to Raleigh earlier that day for an insurance examination. He later said he felt
like he was in a coma. Meanwhile, Dale had undergone an emergency root
canal that morning. They met anyway, mainly to avoid upsetting his mother
and her sister. Even though they were not feeling their best, there was a spark
of interest. The pair decided to meet again. The spark soon became a flame
and romance ensued!

Eventually, the time came for Bob to meet Dale's father. Bob arrived at
the Martin residence, across the street from South Hills: "I was going to a
family friend's wedding with Mr. and Mrs. Martin. Diane and I rode with

143

them because Dale was going to be in the wedding party and had traveled ahead of us. I walked into his house and, of all things, when he shook my hand for the first time, he was on the telephone. So, he held the phone—it wasn't a cell phone—it was a land line. It was one of these things where he held it and shook my hand and kind of mouthed to me, 'Nice to meet you.' So, he was on the phone, and he's been on the phone ever since."

Bob was impressed from the start with David's efficiency. David handled business calls right up until time to leave for the wedding. Then, while Bob and Diane rode with Marilyn to the wedding, David followed them. He had already arranged for Marilyn to stop at a tire shop in Garner and to wait for him there. David planned to drop off his van to have the tires replaced and then ride with his wife, daughter and Bob the remaining distance to the wedding. "He has always shown me that you don't have any wasted motion if you can avoid it," Bob said.

Luckily, Diane worked at the Underwood School just long enough to play matchmaker for Dale and Bob. Diane had been there only a few months, however, when her father asked her to come to work for the family business in the University Apartments leasing office. She started working there when she was pregnant with her first child, David and Marilyn's third grandson, William Boyd Stephenson, III, who arrived in November 1987.

William Boyd Stephenson, III

To better serve their tenants, the leasing office had been moved from 3700 Western Blvd. to the onsite location at 700 Ryan Ct. David converted a one-bedroom apartment into an office and added a room to it so she could keep the baby there. Diane and Will went on to have four more sons, all of which she took to work with her at the apartments. "There was a big pine tree near the office, and we had a basketball goal attached to it and the area fenced off so the kids could play basketball—all five of them. Mom and I worked together," Diane recalled.

June 1987 was a notable month for the Martin Family because David and Marilyn deeded a lot in Triangle Forest to each of their children, so they could all have a home there. Donna's pick, on Donna Place, was a foregone conclusion. David, Jr., Dotty, and Debbie's choices were nearby. Diane recalled how she chose her plot. "I was the last one to choose. I think they kind of knew which one I would choose because it was the plot directly behind the house we grew up in—until I was in the third grade—at 103 Marilyn Circle. We had a screened-in porch that came off the back of the house, and we used to have our birthday parties there on that back porch with the neighborhood kids."

November 1987 was a great month for the Martins for another reason. Exactly two weeks after Diane gave birth to William, Donna gave birth to Sarah "Kristen" Evenson, the Martins' first granddaughter. The number of Martin grandchildren continued to increase and in January 1988, Dotty gave birth to Scott Robert Reintgen, their fourth grandson.

Kristen Evenson, the Martins' first granddaughter, pictured with her father, Eric, was born in November 1987, and in January 1988 their grandson, Scott Reintgen, was born. He is pictured with his grandmother, Marilyn.

Love was in the air as Bob transferred to Nationwide's regional office in Raleigh. Not only would he get more exposure to a corporate setting, but more importantly he would also be closer to Dale. Eventually, he asked Dale to marry him. He planned to ask David and Marilyn for their blessing when the three of them could meet. He approached Marilyn for her blessing about a week before speaking to David and swore her to secrecy. Bob finally asked David for her hand in marriage one evening when the family had gathered to watch "The Sound of Music." They had not watched the musical long before David asked Marilyn if she would mind if he went to sow seed on his land down the street from South Hills. Knowing better than to hold David back from his work, she told him to go ahead. Bob, who had been waiting for an opportunity to catch David alone, offered to help. David took one look at what Bob was wearing—nice clothes and a new pair of Dockers—and hesitated briefly, but he accepted his help. Off they went! About 20 minutes into their work, Bob finally got up the courage to ask permission to marry Dale. David asked him, "What's the most important thing about marriage?" Bob responded with, "That we love each other." David replied it was important that they remain committed to the marriage, because love comes and goes. Relieved at having accomplished his mission, Bob was very happy and was ready to leave the job site. However, David kept him there for a few more hours, pointing first to one area and then another, saying "let's go over here" or "let's go over there." He was having a little fun at his future son-in-law's expense, and Bob's persistence and capacity for hard work were being put to the test! When the men were finished, the new Dockers were ruined, but Bob figured losing them was a small price to pay for getting the green light to marry Dale! The happy day arrived in April 1988. Dale followed in her sisters' footsteps and walked down the aisle at First Baptist Church in Cary.

Bob and Dale were married at
First Baptist Church in Cary, in April 1988.

In another strange coincidence, just as David had met Diane's future father-in-law years earlier, it turned out he had also met Dale's future father-in-law 14 years before she tied the knot. Bob's father, Herb Dascombe, an executive with Nationwide Insurance, learned early in 1974 that he was being transferred from the Pittsburgh, PA, area to Raleigh. He started house hunting, and one of the houses he considered was the Martins' former home at 103 Marilyn Circle, which David and Marilyn had recently placed on the market. Mr. Dascombe determined that he could not afford that house, but he later remembered David telling him, "Just trust that God will take care of you."

CHAPTER 31

Changes at Martin Properties

Plans fail for lack of counsel, but with many advisers they succeed. (Proverbs 15:22 NIV)

Debbie spent a brief period in Colorado before she married her fiancé, a man with a self -described "cultural Jewish background," in September 1989, in Mohawk, NY. After they married, they lived in Manhattan. David, Jr., married Kelly Garten a few weeks later in Cary. Both marriages ended in divorce some years later.

While in New York, Debbie took a job with Kansai Paint (America), Inc. "God gave me opportunities," Debbie said. "I got to work for this billion-dollar industry. I was an account executive, and, like my Dad, I just kind of made my way. I found my positions and built myself up." In true Martin fashion, Debbie worked long hours. "The girl that worked for me had a four-year degree and was my assistant," she said. "God let me do a lot of unique things, but I still have that regret that I didn't graduate from college."

Though some difficult times had come to David, Jr.'s and Debbie's marriages, God continued to bless David and Marilyn with grandchildren. In February 1989, Diane gave birth to David "Martin" Stephenson, their fifth grandson. Dotty gave birth to Patrick Lee Reintgen, their sixth grandson, in May and Dale gave birth to her parents' seventh grandson, Addison Beatty Dascombe, in November of the same year.

David "Martin" Stephenson

Patrick Lee Reintgen

Addison Beatty Dascombe

During Dale's pregnancy, she and Bob initially discussed her returning to work at South Hills after their son was born. However, as she came closer to her due date, they decided she would be a stay-at-home mom. David asked Bob if he would be willing to come to work for Martin Properties in Dale's place. However, after thinking it over, David told Bob he wanted input from the Martin children first. Bob was a little relieved. He had recently been promoted to claims manager at Nationwide. He was managing eight claims adjusters and making good money for a person under 30. Nationwide's management had told Bob that if he passed some additional insurance classes, received various insurance designations, and was willing to relocate, he had a path to advancement in the company. "Mobility, however, was communicated. They said, 'You can't stay in Raleigh forever. You're probably going to have to go to Columbus, Ohio.

You're probably going to have to go all across the country as you climb that ladder, because that is just the corporate way,'" Bob reminisced.

David knew he needed to fill Dale's position after her baby was born, so he brought David, Jr. into the office for about two weeks to see how he fared in that environment. At the end of the two-week period, he and David, Jr. mutually agreed the younger man was not a good match for the position. He did not like working in the office; he would rather be solving problems by working with his hands. David, Jr. later operated a collectibles business at the mall, but he eventually closed it. He has worked in the Martin Properties Maintenance Division for over 30 years.

Soon after his son's trial period, David left Bob a voicemail. He had spoken to his children, and they wanted him to approach Bob about the position again. The two men met several times for lunch. During those lunches, they talked about their business philosophies and what Bob's job would entail. Sometimes their wives chauffeured them around to various places while they talked. "It wasn't an instant decision, but eventually we decided that I would join the family business," Bob said. However, he wanted to stay at Nationwide until he reached his fifth year of employment with the company, so he could become fully vested in Nationwide's pension plan. David told him he could start work in either two weeks or 90 days, whichever worked best for him. Bob's superiors agreed he could leave in 90 days. They were sorry to lose him, but they recognized his new job would provide an opportunity for him to grow professionally while remaining in the Triangle area. "We joke that I got Dale pregnant and took her job and then kept her pregnant so she wouldn't come back," Bob said.

CHAPTER 32

Godly Influence

He must hold firmly to the trustworthy message as it has been taught, so that he can encourage others by sound doctrine and refute those who oppose it. (Titus 1:9 NIV)

When Bob started working for Martin Properties in October 1989, he hoped to bring with him the business practices he had used during his time at Nationwide. David graciously allowed Bob to move into what had been his own office. David himself moved into the smaller office next door previously occupied by Dale. Bob said his father-in-law knew that in his new position Bob would be a manager not just of things but of people, and he wanted Bob to have the space necessary to do his job. "So I started in that corner, and I literally touched everything in the office," Bob said. "Dale helped me. We basically cleaned and organized a bunch of things. I found all sorts of things I needed to understand about the business and the learning process began."

Bob spent the year 1990 becoming acclimated to life in a family business. In the meantime, David's close friend, Dr. Harvey Duke, the pastor of First Baptist Church in Cary, told him he planned to buy a house for his wife, June. They had lived in the parsonage, which was in dire need of repair, since they began serving the church in 1969. When David asked Dr. Duke how he planned to pay for the house, Dr. Duke responded that he planned to get a 20 or 30-year mortgage loan. David stopped him right there and sold him and Mrs. Duke on the idea that a 15-year-loan would be best for them. That way, Dr. Duke could retire in a few years and, if anything happened to him, Mrs. Duke would not have a mortgage payment. David went a step further and talked to their loan officer at Fidelity Bank to ensure the Dukes received the most favorable terms possible. David proudly related that some years later "the Dukes came to tell us they paid off the house in 11-and-a-half-years."

In April 1990, Martin Properties hired Sue Lee as receptionist and office assistant. She recalled that during the early days of her career one of Mr. Martin's employees was terminally ill. Sue recounted the following story about how David helped the young man: "Mr. Martin, at his expense, added a bedroom onto the employee's home for his comfort. He would have me pick up groceries and deliver them to this young man. This has left a lasting impression in my mind about how kind and considerate Mr. Martin is." Over the 27 years Sue has worked at Martin Properties, she has been promoted several times. Today she is the human resources and accounting manager for the business. Over the years she has watched Mr. Martin help countless people in need and is extremely grateful for how kind he has always been to her own family.

Two new grandchildren also helped put a smile on David's face in 1990. David Jr's. wife, Kelly, gave birth to their first child and the Martin's second granddaughter, Julia Lynne Martin, in September, and Diane gave birth to her and Will's third son, Parker Ross Stephenson, in December. The birth of Parker brought the number of grandsons the Martins had to eight. David and Marilyn did not have to wait long for more grandchildren to come along. The following year saw the birth of Dale and Bob's second child, Landon Perry Dascombe, in January; Debbie and her husband's first child and the Martin's third granddaughter, Alexandra Leigh Weintraub, in mid-August; and David Jr. and Kelly's second child, Jillian Taylor Martin, in late August. By the end of 1991, the Martins had nine grandsons and four granddaughters!

Julia Lynne Martin   *Parker Ross Stephenson*   *Landon Perry Dascombe*

Alexandra Leigh Weintraub

Jillian Taylor Martin

Another reason for the Martins to smile in 1990 was the return of their daughter Dotty to North Carolina. After eight years in the ministry and much contemplation and prayer, Jeff decided on a career change. He, Dotty, and their three children moved back the Triangle Area. Jeff enrolled in the dental school at UNC-Chapel Hill, graduating in 1994. He currently operates a successful dental practice with locations in north Raleigh and Apex. Upon her return to North Carolina, Dotty worked for UNC Hospital for six years. Since she left her position at the hospital, she has helped Jeff run both offices. Dotty added that she has also inherited her father's work ethic. She works long hours in her position as office manager to ensure no detail is overlooked and every aspect of Reintgen Family Dentistry runs smoothly.

Besides the birth of three new grandchildren and the return of Dotty and her family to the area, 1991 was also significant due to the drive spearheaded by David's friend J. Russell Capps to get permission from the former members of the Wake County Taxpayers Association to resurrect it. David, a long-time conservative, was very supportive of resurrecting the Taxpayers Association and still contributes to the organization today. Capps was later elected a Republican member of the

North Carolina General Assembly from 1996-2006. He represented the NC. 50th House District until state lawmakers redrew the districts; then he represented the 41st district.

While David did try to serve his community in various ways politically, his first love was to God and furthering the message of his church. He was appointed to represent First Baptist Church as a messenger to the annual Southern Baptist Convention (SBC) several times over the years, particularly during the time Dr. Duke was the minister at First Baptist. During this meeting, representatives or "messengers" from member churches gather to confer and determine the programs, policies, and budget of the SBC for the coming year. In 1985, David and his son-in-law Eric were both messengers to the SBC for their respective churches. They flew together to Dallas, the convention site that year; drove to the convention; cast their votes for Charles Stanley to be president; then immediately flew back home!

Additionally, as an active and involved Southern Baptist layman, David wanted to ensure that the graduates from Southeastern Baptist Theological Seminary have experience sharing the gospel before being sent to the mission field. He was one of many people who pushed for the seminary to institute changes leading in that direction. In June 1992, at age 64, David was elected a messenger to the SBC, held in Indianapolis. Bruce Russell, Sr., the brother of David's friend and dry-cleaning customer, Charles Russell, has served on the seminary's Board of Visitors with David for many years and remembered David was "very cooperative and supportive" of the seminary's efforts to train men and women to spread the gospel.

CHAPTER 33

The Maestro at Work

One person gives freely, yet gains even more; another withholds
unduly yet comes to poverty. (Proverbs 11:24 NIV)

While David was busy promoting the seminary in 1992, the country was
in the Savings and Loan Crisis, which had its beginnings in 1986 and
lasted well into the next decade, finally easing in 1995. At that time, it
marked the worst banking collapse since the Great Depression. By 1989,
more than 1,000 of the nation's savings and loans (S&L's) had failed, and
by the end of 1995 more than half of them were no longer in existence.
Eventually, the Federal Savings and Loan Insurance Corporation went
bankrupt.[61] The origins of the crisis were complex, and the necessary
remedies were complicated and expensive. Before it was over, the
crisis had cost the S&L Industry $28 billion and American taxpayers
$132 billion. In the end, the Resolution Trust Corporation (RTC) was
established to sell off the assets of the failed institutions.[62]

Meanwhile, David, unlike many other developers, had not rushed
to buy land and take out loans with the S&L's. He had been saving his
money and consequently had the capital available to pick up some of
the pieces of land and property the RTC had for sale. In 1992, David hit

---

[61] Savings and Loan Crisis 1980-1989," The Federal Reserve, November 22, 2013,
https://www.federalreservehistory.org/essays/savings_and_loan_crisis

[62] Kimberly Amadeo, "Savings and Loan Crisis Explained: How Congress Created
the Greatest Bank Collapse Since the Depression," *The Balance*, https://www.
thebalance.com/savings-and-loans-crises-causes-cost-3306035, updated July 17,
2017.

a bonanza. He made about 20 purchases at incredible prices! He also acquired several other foreclosed properties from banks.

Bob, who by that time had worked for David about three years, explained how he watched as Martin Properties profited from David's purchases: "I was pretty much a briefcase boy. I had manila folders. I had contracts. I had no idea what he was really doing, other than that I was trying to help him stay organized. But when he bought a property, for instance, for $19,000, years later that property sold for $400,000. So, one thing Mr. Martin taught me during that era was you make your money when you buy it. It's kind of a play on words. It's with anything. I could buy a bottle of water for 2 cents, on sale, and then I could go out to the fairgrounds, put it on ice, and sell it for $2. It's how you buy it that counts. So here he was buying all this land. I didn't know the value of land then. The reason he could buy land at auctions was because he had the capital on hand and other bidders didn't. When they couldn't raise the capital, they'd have to drop out of the bidding."

One prime example of David employing this strategy was his purchase of the Plantation Square Shopping Center in North Raleigh. David acquired this property from Southern National Bank at an auction. Bob tagged along the day of the auction to observe David in action. David's bid was not the highest, but he jockeyed for position to be the back-up bidder. Bob explained there are two types of auctions—absolute and reserve. In an absolute auction, the auctioneer sells to the highest bidder. When the bidding is over, that person pays a premium to the auctioneer and the transaction is complete. Plantation Square was bought at a reserve auction, however. In this type of auction, the auctioneer takes the highest bid, but it is subject to bank approval. A furniture retailer had placed the highest bid, and David placed the back-up bid. The Southern National officers could not accept the furniture retailer's bid, however, because the amount he offered to pay upfront was too low. The auctioneer, acting as a go-between for Southern National and the retailer tried to broker a deal, but the furniture retailer wanted a "steal" and the negotiations were unsuccessful.

In the meantime, David had not been idle. He wisely told the auctioneer that if the bank and the bidder were not able to do business, he would like another chance to talk to him. "So, Mr. Martin worked it," Bob said. "I observed as the bank and the auctioneer, who then became a real estate agent, talked. It wasn't a one encounter talk, but after several encounters, several weeks, several moving parts, the bank, Southern National Bank, sold Plantation Square to the Martin Family Trust for $1.3 million. The original borrower that the bank foreclosed on had over $4 million in it. So, it was a work-out deal. The reason the bank sold it for $1.3 million was because it was the best price they could get at the time, and the government was telling these banks to stop owning real estate." Bob also said the advantage of buying the shopping center from the bank was that David did not have to initially borrow money to get it. He had enough capital for a down payment. Southern National did lend him the money for the balance. "They were willing to give us a loan because they liked Mr. Martin's strength," Bob said. "They knew that we would perform, and we had the ability to make that monthly payment. So, it was a really good deal. Little did I know how good of a deal it was at the time, because, keep in mind, I had been in the business for three years. I just had a front row seat watching the maestro at work: David Martin."

One thing David insisted upon when he took out the loan with Southern National was that the loan have a term of 15 years. "I think I have always profited because whenever I take out a loan it's for 15 years," he said. Plantation Square was not an instant success, but its value has grown steadily over the years, and after renovations were completed in 2015, its appraised value jumped to $6.9 million.

Plantation Square Shopping Center as it looks today.

"That's just an example," Bob said. "But '92 was the catalyst for the family to expand, and when it expanded it took more effort and more energy. I used to be called the mall manager, but the mall manager at

South Hills doesn't fare too well with a tenant at Plantation Square, so that's when I became the senior vice-president at Martin Properties."

When Bob took over Dale's job, Martin Properties was a much smaller entity, comprised mainly of South Hills Mall and Plaza, University Apartments, and the trust that David had set up for his children and grandchildren. That trust contained only 15 acres of land along I-40 behind Crossroads Shopping Center. With the acquisition of 20 additional properties—including Lakeview Office Park in Cary and the Salem Center Professional Building in Apex—the Martin Family's wealth increased and, along with it, Bob's responsibilities as manager of the Martins' business portfolio.

Kendell Walker Stephenson

The year 1992 was capped off for David and Marilyn with the birth in December of their tenth grandson, Will and Diane's fourth child, Kendell Walker Stephenson.

CHAPTER 34

Time with the Grandkids

These commandments that I give you today are to be on your hearts. Impress them on your children. Talk about them when you sit at home and when you walk along the road, when you lie down and when you get up. (Deuteronomy 6:6-7 NIV)

By the end of 1992, David and Marilyn had 14 grandchildren. All of them have stories about the time they have spent with their grandfather. Sometimes he showed his love for them by doing things for them. Other times he expressed his affection by teaching them a spiritual lesson or helping them develop a strong work ethic and skills they could use later in life.

John Evenson was present in 1985, when he was two-and-a-half years old, as concrete was poured for the sidewalk at the entrance to the South Hills Mall addition. "I remember my mom putting my hands in the concrete, and the prints are still there till this day," he said. In 1987, when he was five years old, David and some employees went to John's parents' home and built a fort for him in the backyard. John recalled the event: "They framed it out and built it up in one day and put the roof on it. It was a normal workday, and they built it up specifically for me. I vividly remember Granddaddy and Ray Cooke being there. My dad and I painted it camouflage. It had a porch on it, windows and doors. I remember it was 1987 because the sign we had on it said: 'Established, July 4, 1987.' He built me a fort in the middle of the work week. For somebody like him, who never stops working, that's kind of a remarkable moment." Those were fun times for John, and he recalled that every time he saw his grandfather, David called him Big John, after the country music singer Jimmy Dean's song, "Big John."

Another of David's grandsons, Addison Dascombe, recalled some of his favorite memories with his grandfather. Addison said he enjoyed the times David took him out for pizza. When attending Addison's sporting events, David almost always got some laughs by saying or doing something funny. He added that David was the kind of grandfather who would get on a bicycle or scooter belonging to one of his grandchildren and ride it around the neighborhood!

Besides creating good memories with his grandchildren, it was important to David that he speak to them about spiritual things. One day while his grandsons John Evenson and Matt Reintgen were at their grandparents' house for a visit, he asked John to read Psalm 1.[63]

Matt Reintgen

John Evenson

David began teaching John and Matt about the truth of the Bible when they were about the ages of eight and six, respectively.

---

[63] Blessed is the one who does not walk in step with the wicked or stand in the way that sinners take or sit in the company of mockers, but whose delight is in the law of the Lord, and who meditates on his law day and night. That person is like a tree planted by streams of water, which yields its fruit in season and whose leaf does not wither—whatever they do prospers. Not so the wicked! They are like chaff that the wind blows away. Therefore, the wicked will not stand in the judgment, nor sinners in the assembly of the righteous. For the Lord watches over the way of the righteous, but the way of the wicked leads to destruction. (Psalm 1:1-6, NIV)

When he asked John if he knew what the passage meant, John said he did not understand it. David had the boys get in his car. John recalled the rest of the experience: "It was before we were ever driving, and we stopped by a wheat field. He held a wheat stalk in his hand and said when the farmer takes the wheat he blows away the chaff, and the wheat stays behind. 'You see that? The chaff blows away and the wheat stays behind.' He explained that those people who follow the truth of Christianity and its teachings would stand firm because it lasts forever, but those people who followed other teachings or ways would be blown away. I'll never forget that. It may even be the most vivid early memory I have."

David spent time with his granddaughters too. His granddaughter Alexandra Weintraub treasures the time he drove rather fast through Triangle Forest while they looked at Christmas lights! Alexandra also recalled that her grandfather used the same Bible passage he had used to instruct John and Matt to impart a slightly different spiritual lesson to her.

Alexandra Weintraub

She learned to read early, and when she was six years old, he had her read Psalm 1 to him. David then discussed with Alexandra what this passage meant. During their discussion, he impressed on her that she should not socialize with wicked people and should always follow the way of truth. Afterward, he made a notation in his Bible next to the passage and recorded the date she read it to him, August 10, 1998. Like his mother had done for him, and as he did with own his children, David also made sure to impress upon all his grandchildren the importance of attending church regularly.

In addition to making good memories with his grandchildren and teaching them invaluable spiritual lessons, David also endeavored to impart to them the importance of having a good work ethic. He particularly wanted to be sure his grandsons knew how to work hard and to take proper care of the family's property. One day when John was in fifth grade, David took him to work at the mall. John's job that day was to scrape paint off the pink tiles in one of the back rooms of what became the Tuesday Morning store. David also assigned John the task of scraping paint off the outside of some of the windows. Before they left for the day, he had John step back and look at the property. He told him: "You see this! This is yours! You need to take care of it!"

David's grandson Martin Stephenson said he started working with his grandfather at about the age of eight or nine years old. On one occasion, he and a couple of his cousins worked with their grandfather as he tilled a field at South Hills Mall in preparation for planting grass seed and putting in fertilizer.

*Scott Reintgen, 12, standing next to a sign for a then
prospective K&S Cafeteria in Garner, NC.*

Before David added the seed, he had them pick up the sticks and rocks that the tiller dredged up. Sometimes, they worked in one spot for a long while. "I just remember him tilling and tilling over and over again, and we were thinking, 'Can you not till anymore?'" Martin said. "That's where I learned to work hard." Later, when Martin played basketball for Guilford College, a small liberal arts college in Greensboro, NC, he looked back on this experience with gratitude. "I remember when Coach would yell at us and have us do things over and over. I would remember my grandfather and push through it."

A permanent memory of David sporting gray hair, bushy eyebrows, and a flannel shirt with pockets stuffed full of notes are the first memories that come to mind about his granddaddy, for Scott Reintgen. Like his cousins before him, Scott remembers riding with David to various construction sites. When there, Scott either worked alongside his grandfather or David showed Scott how something was done.

Martin Stephenson remembers tilling a field
with his grandfather at the age of 8.

On one occasion, when Scott was 12 or 13 years old, David cut his arm while they were working together; however, he did not stop to bandage it. Finally, Scott asked him, "You realize that you're bleeding, right?" David responded rather nonchalantly that he would take care of the cut after he was finished working. "He's an immensely hard worker." Scott said. "You had to know what you were getting into when you got into the truck with Granddaddy."

Addison recalled that he began working with his grandfather at about the same age as his cousins. Much of the work involved driving tractors, filling in holes, and repairing ceilings and roofs at South Hills Mall.

"One day I'll buy a house and have a family, and I'll know how to do some of the things that need to be done to it." Though Alexandra did not work for her grandfather like her male cousins did, she said he did take her to his office and tell her about his work.

While nearly all his grandsons worked with him at different times, either at the mall or at one of his other properties, David by no means "worked them to death." He would take time to teach them things, too. He once took about four hours of his day to give Addison driving lessons in the South Hills parking lot. "I'll never forget my Dad's face when, as a 12-year-old-boy, I drove up in my Granddaddy's pickup truck," he said. David also praised his grandchildren whenever they came up with a good idea and bragged about their ingenuity to everyone he met.

David's efforts to impart a strong work ethic in his grandchildren have paid off. John Evenson now owns and operates Southern Flyway Outfitters, selling his own unique and very successful invention—an ingenious decoy raft for duck hunters. Addison Dascombe had been working as a senior financial analyst with AJ Wealth in New York City, before recently accepting a position as a private wealth advisor for Regions Bank in Charlotte, NC. Scott Reintgen, a former English teacher, is now a successful author of young adult science fiction, with all three books of his *Nyxia* trilogy already published. He is moving forward with plans for at least four more novels. Martin Stephenson worked for several years after college graduation in management for a local landscaping company. In the fall of 2015, he joined Martin Properties as Maintenance Service Manager. Alexandra Weintraub Brown also attributes the reason she continues to work hard and put forth her best effort in the service industry to the work ethic her grandfather instilled in her.

CHAPTER 35

Blessings at Work and Home

He and all his family were devout and God-fearing; he gave generously to those in need and prayed to God regularly. (Acts 10:2 NIV)

The 1990s were a fruitful time for the Martin Family as David and Marilyn were blessed with still more grandchildren. In March 1993, David Jr.'s wife, Kelly, gave birth to Kimberley Jon-Hope "Jonni" Martin, their fifth granddaughter. Debbie gave birth to Samantha Eden Weintraub later that year, the Martin's sixth granddaughter. The following years saw the births of Skyler Marilyn Dascombe, Bob and Dale's only daughter and the Martin's seventh granddaughter, in 1994; Dalton Montgomery Weintraub, Debbie's only son and the Martin's eleventh grandson, in 1996; Cameron Brooks Stephenson, the Martins twelfth grandson and Diane and Will's youngest child, later in September 1996; and, rounding off the decade, William Camden Dascombe, Bob and Dale's youngest child, in 1998. By the end of the 1990's the Martins had a grand total of thirteen grandsons and seven granddaughters!

Jonni   *Samantha*   *Skyler*

Dalton   *Cameron*   *Camden*

As mentioned previously, in 1987 David had given each of his children a parcel of land on which to build a home. David, Jr. built his house in 1990; Dale built hers in 1991. Donna, Dotty, and Diane each built their houses in 1994. Debbie never built a house on her land, and eventually her parents helped her buy a home in Fayetteville. Each of the five Martin children who built homes in Triangle Forest served as their own contractors. As might be expected, David assisted them with the construction process. Donna, who designed her home, said her father made her sweep and clean the site every night after they stopped working! A harrowing and somewhat hilarious incident occurred while David was preparing the site for Donna's house. The brakes went out on the large earth-mover he was driving. As he zigzagged down the hill to slow down, he knocked out all the mailboxes along the street until he came to a stop!

The year 1993 marked the 30th Anniversary of South Hills Mall. The occasion was marked by a special ceremony including the Mayor of Cary, Koka Booth. A display depicting the history of the mall was erected for the whole community to see.

Cary Mayor Koka Booth, David Martin, Sr. President, Martin Properties and his wife, Marilyn Martin, pose at a historical display during the South Hills 30th anniversary celebration.

Additionally, David hired a bakery to make a huge cake in the shape of the mall and the plaza. This unusual but delicious creation was enjoyed by the mall customers as well as Martin family members and special guests.

In 1995, members of the Martin Family Trust were faced with an important decision regarding Plantation Square Shopping Center. John Tsai, owner of the Sesame Wok Chinese restaurant, wrote a letter addressed to Bob, the trust representative, requesting permission to serve alcohol during the Christmas Holiday Season, including New Year's Day. He made this request, he stated, because he was losing business in the evenings to two nearby Chinese restaurants that offered buffets, which Sesame Wok did not. He felt that serving alcohol would give him a much-needed edge.

In a memo to David and the members of the trust, Bob told them they needed to discuss how a Christian-based business, which is also a commercial landlord, should address this "delicate issue." He continued that if the members wanted him to create a policy that allowed their restaurant tenants to sell alcohol, then these tenants would have to meet very specific requirements. Among these requirements, Bob suggested, would be that any restaurant that wanted to sell alcohol be duly licensed by the state. Also, only unfortified wine or beer would be sold and only with a full dinner. Furthermore, the business would be required to donate 10 percent of their alcohol sales to a trust-approved non-profit organization working toward the restriction or elimination of alcohol sales. Finally, the restaurant owners would be required to obtain adequate liability insurance for themselves as well as the trust.

In David's mind, the issue had already been settled. He had never allowed a business to sell alcohol on any of the family's properties. Furthermore, when representatives of a brewery had wanted to rent space for a fundraiser, he turned them down as well. In the end, arguments for both sides were considered, but the trust members decided not to allow alcohol to be sold on any of their properties. Several reasons were cited for their decision: First and foremost, they wanted to honor God. Additionally, their father had always admonished them to stay clear of alcohol, because alcohol, if abused, can destroy people's lives. Finally, they felt that no organization that fights against the irresponsible use of alcohol would want money donated from a restaurant that sells alcohol.

With that issue settled, the Martins faced another challenge. In October 1996, Debbie and her husband separated. She and her three children moved in with her father and mother. David and Marilyn had misgivings about her husband before she married him, but they were very supportive of her when the relationship soured. "My parents never said, 'I told you so,'" Debbie said. "When I came to my senses, like the Prodigal Son's father,[64] they welcomed me back, and they helped me."

---

[64] Jesus continued: "There was a man who had two sons. The younger one said to his father, 'Father, give me my share of the estate.' So he divided his property between them. "Not long after that, the younger son got together all he had, set off for a distant country and there squandered his wealth in wild living. After he had spent everything, there was a severe famine in that whole country, and he began to be in need. So he went and hired himself out to a citizen of that country, who sent him to his fields to feed pigs. He longed to fill his stomach with the pods that the pigs were eating, but no one gave him anything. "When he came to his senses, he said, 'How many of my father's hired servants have food to spare, and here I am starving to death! I will set out and go back to my father and say to him: Father, I have sinned against heaven and against you. I am no longer worthy to be called your son; make me like one of your hired servants.' So, he got up and went to his father. "But while he was still a long way off, his father saw him and was filled with compassion for him; he ran to his son, threw his arms around him and kissed him." "The son said to him, 'Father, I have sinned against heaven and against you. I am no longer worthy to be called your son.' "But the father said to his servants, 'Quick! Bring the best robe and put it on him. Put a ring on his finger and sandals on his feet. Bring the fattened calf and kill it. Let's have a feast and celebrate. For this son of mine was dead and is alive again; he was lost and is found.' So they began to celebrate." (Luke 15:11-24 (NIV)

David built a kitchen in the basement of his home and ensured the rooms were fit for his daughter and grandchildren to live in. He also gave her a key so she could secure their living area when they were out. Now that she was back in the Triangle region and had no child support from her estranged husband, she immediately began looking for a job to support herself and her children. David, influenced by watching his own mother's struggles, had developed a strong desire for helping single mothers in tough circumstances. When it came to Debbie and his grandchildren, however, he truly excelled in his generosity. He felt he could best meet their needs by providing for them so Debbie could stay home with her children during their formative years. Debbie recalled how he presented the idea to her: "He said, 'You're doing a great job raising your children. I want you to stay home and raise them,' and I said, 'I can't, I've got to get a job. I'm a single parent now.' He said, 'Look, I can help you and you can put your focus on your children, or you can be prideful and never see them.'" When Debbie agreed to accept his help, she broke down and cried out of gratitude for her parents' generosity. Debbie's divorce was finalized in March 1997.

When Debbie's youngest child, Dalton, turned three, she took him to work with her at University Apartments, where she worked alongside Diane and her mother. "Dad enabled us to have an environment where the kids could be at work. I grew up that way and it was wonderful. It was a wonderful opportunity for them," she said. Debbie and her children lived with her parents for six and a half years. Even after she remarried a few years later, David sent a monthly stipend to her children and continued to do so for years afterward.

Amid the change from being empty nesters to having a grown daughter and grandchildren move back home, David was pressing forward to ensure South Hills Mall had family-friendly businesses that would create unique experiences for their patrons. He had always had a vision for a cafeteria at the mall where he and others could have a home-cooked meal in an alcohol-free environment and enjoy themselves with their families. He did not just dream about it; he built it! In 1998, the K&S Cafeteria opened its doors in a building David had built specifically to meet the needs of the staff and customers. He leased this building to the owner, Harry Smith, with terms too favorable to refuse.

On hand for the K&S grand opening and ribbon cutting ceremony were (Left to Right) Cary Mayor Koka Booth, Bob Dascombe, Senior V.P., Martin Properties; Harry Smith, Owner, K&S Cafeteria; David Martin, Sr., President, Martin Properties; and Howard Johnson, President of Cary Chamber of Commerce.

David himself quickly became a fixture at the cafeteria and still eats there regularly. He greets the workers and socializes with all the customers he knows—a good-sized portion of the clientele considering how long he has been a Cary resident. Jerry Miller recalled the following about times he has seen David at the cafeteria: "When I eat at the cafeteria—whoever I am sitting with—he comes by and he will ask every one of them what their names are." He added that David also asks for their wives' names and the name of the church they attend. When he finds out he writes this information as well as their numbers in his day timer.

David always insists on picking up the tab for his friends as well as the business associates he invites to the cafeteria. Even if he is unable to join them, David routinely asks many of his friends, new and old, to go ahead and eat without him—then to leave the bill with the cashier for him to settle later. Additionally, each year he sponsors a lunch for the surviving members of his high school class in the cafeteria's private dining room. He also offers to pay for employees, friends, and members of his church to have a meal with their loved ones when there has been a death in their family. Dr. Frank F. Yarborough, whose parents helped

David when he was a boy said this about how David offered to pay for his family's lunch in their time of sorrow: "David is one of those people who never forgets what other people do for them. My first wife's mother, Natalie Beddingfield, was one of those people who had given him jobs when he was young. When she died he attended the funeral and invited the whole family—everybody that was at the funeral—over here to K&S, gave them the back room, and paid for everybody's meal. He just never forgets anybody that's ever done anything for him. When my first wife and brother died, he did the same thing. Nobody contacted him. I didn't call him. He called me and invited my whole family over."

Today, the cafeteria is known as the D&S Cafeteria. Current owners, Sylvester and Diane Smith, left their jobs in corporate America and began helping the previous owner, Sylvester's brother Harry, with the cafeteria in 1998. In 2010, they took over ownership of the establishment and came up with the new name—hence the D&S cafeteria was born.[65]

---

[65] Sue Stock, "K&S is now D&S," *The News and Observer*, pg, 1, Section B.

CHAPTER 36

A Man and His Tractor

You shall not steal. (Exodus 20:15 NIV)

One constant about the shopping center industry is that it is always changing to meet the needs of the tenants and customers. In 1997, Burlington Coat Factory, South Hill's largest tenant, requested and was granted more space at the north end of the mall. Some smaller stores were removed to make room for its expansion. The change marked the beginning of the process of de-malling at South Hills, though at the time neither David nor Bob referred to it by that term. Within six years, however, "de-malling" would become a familiar word to South Hills tenants and customers. In a 2002 interview for the *Cary News* concerning changes at the mall, David told the reporter, "You either change or you die. That's the way it is with anything."[66]

After realizing his dream of building a cafeteria, David had another victory of sorts the following year. In 1999, he recovered his Kubota tractor that had been stolen while in use at South Hills back in 1992. He had filed a police report, but law enforcement's efforts to locate the tractor were unsuccessful. Not easily deterred, David was persistent in his search for the tractor and described his mentality about finding it. "Once I set my mind to do something, I stick with it, and I was determined to get my tractor back," he said. "So, every Sunday for seven years and two months, I checked the newspaper for farm equipment for sale in the classifieds section. I knew at some point that tractor was going

---

[66] Megan Jones, "South Hills Plans Face lift: Small stores to be consolidated into fewer 'big-box' retailers", pg. 15A.

to come up for sale, and I was watching for it." When he read one Sunday that a Kubota tractor was for sale and that it had a John Deere mower deck instead of its original one, David knew there was a good chance it was his missing tractor. He still had the original deck in storage. As soon as he could, he took Bob with him to see the tractor, and, just as he suspected, it was his missing property.

David, in December of 2016, on the Kubota tractor
that he found seven years after it was stolen.

David called the police, and he confronted the seller. Bob recalled the man had a very bad attitude, saying, "You own half of Cary and now you're bothering me with wanting this tractor back!" David explained what happened next: "The man who was selling it claimed he paid $3,500 for it and showed me a receipt for a cashier's check. The police said I couldn't take the tractor. Well, I have been around the block a bit, and I sized the man up. It didn't look right to me. So, I went down to the bank and had them investigate that cashier's check. Sure enough, it was not what he had presented it to be. He had it drawn up just a few weeks before. So, I showed that to the police, and after seven years and two months of looking, I took my tractor home that very day. Some people probably wonder why I would waste all that time and energy for a tractor. I've got enough money to buy another one after all. Well, it's the principle of the matter that's important to me. That man stole my tractor. He took something that did not belong to him, and he broke God's law. I just couldn't let that go by without doing something. That tractor was my property, and I am responsible to God to be a good steward of that property." He added that if he had not found the tractor, he would still be looking for it because he was not going to give up trying to find it.

On March 15 of the same year, Lydia Cammann was hired to work for Martin Properties and is still employed there as the office assistant. She keeps David's daily calendar and assists him with leasing and other projects. Lydia said that during the 20 years she has worked for David, she has found that he is better at multi-tasking than most people. "I've seen him going back and forth between two phone calls on his cell phone and one on his land line with little apparent difficulty." In addition to her job responsibilities for David, she also supports Bob Dascombe and Sue Lee in their current roles as general property manager and human resources/accounting manager, respectively.

Lydia continued that David has always been very fair, caring, and family-oriented while she has worked for him. She related the following story to illustrate how he had demonstrated those characteristics: "When I first started working for Martin Properties, I worked part-time, job sharing with another employee. I worked from 8 a.m. till noon, and then left to visit my mother in a local nursing home so I could feed her lunch. Mr. Martin was always very supportive of my situation and later, when I began working full-time, he put it into my contract that I would get a long lunch—an hour-and-a-half—so I would have enough time to visit her before returning to work. Mr. Martin always asked about my mother, and the day she died, he called me on my cell phone and prayed with me."

Lydia added that working for David has helped her to learn to never be afraid to ask questions and to go straight to the top if necessary to get answers or to solve a problem. "I have been able to apply this concept not only in my professional life, but also in my personal life. He has always encouraged me to put God first in every aspect of my life and to 'never, ever give up'. I also admire him for being quick to apologize if he believes he has made a mistake. Additionally, he has taught me the meaning of true gratitude. He has never forgotten any of the people who helped him along the way, and never passes up the opportunity to show kindness to those folks when they or any of their relatives visit our office."

Last but not least, Lydia noted that her 20-year length of service makes her a "baby" as far as her fellow Martin Properties employees are concerned. Bob and Sue, her managers, have worked for the company for 30 and 29 years, respectively. Before his passing in early 2017, Vernon Parrish, along with Ray Cooke, may have been one of David's longest-serving employees. A maintenance technician extraordinaire, Vernon was employed by Martin Properties for at least 35 years, and his father also worked for David. Obviously, Vernon is greatly missed. David always maintained that "Vernon could fix anything but a broken heart!" The loyalty that David has inspired in those who work for him says volumes about his character and the company he has built.

CHAPTER 37

The Purse Snatcher

Learn to do right; seek justice. Defend the oppressed.
Take up the cause of the fatherless; plead the
case of the widow. (Isaiah 1:17 NIV)

Marilyn decided in 2000, after the University Apartments office changed to a computerized bookkeeping system, that it was time to retire. Her duties as head of the residential division of Martin Properties fell on Diane, who by that time had already worked in the University Apartments office for almost 13 years.

Mrs. Martin's retirement was not the only change occurring in the Martins' life. Debbie's life was changing in the best way possible. While Debbie lived in New York City, she had begun to study the Bible. She rededicated her life to Christ, was baptized, and became a member of the New York City Church of Christ. The change in her life was evident when she moved in with her parents and began attending a sister church in Raleigh, the Triangle Church of Christ. In 2001, her friend and fellow church member, Anne Patterson, introduced her to Stephen "Steve" Salek, a young doctoral student. Anne chose the two to teach the combined first- and second-grade Kids Kingdom Sunday school classes. Mrs. Patterson figured the two would end up either really loving or really disliking each other since they were so different! As it turned out, Steve had no interest in a romantic relationship with a mother of three. The two initially became best friends and dated other people who were part of a sister congregation, The Fayetteville Church, in Fayetteville, NC. Those dating relationships did not result in engagements, and though

Steve had moved to take a job as an instructor at Fayetteville State University, the two remained close. Before long it became evident that Steve was the type of man who could be a good husband as well as fill the role of a father to her children. In his spare time, Steve volunteered to help the children of Fort Bragg and Pope Air Force military families who had at least one parent deployed to the Middle East. He spent time with them and took them on trips to places such as the North Carolina State Aquarium in Wilmington, NC, among others.

Steve and Debbie began dating in August 2002, but Debbie was cautious, telling him, "If my family doesn't like you, I'm not going near you." Debbie reasoned, "I made a vow to listen to the people who knew me, and if God gave me a second chance, I would take their advice because I didn't the first time." Steve responded by telling her, "Oh my gosh, Debbie! That's such a scary thing to tell a guy." But as God designed it, he had nothing to worry about. Debbie's parents liked him, and they were engaged by Christmas 2002. When Steve asked her father for Debbie's hand in marriage, David made it easy for him. Before he could say anything, David said, "Looks like you found yourself a wife!"

Change was not happening only for Debbie. When David opened South Hills, he was one of a few retail pioneers in Cary. Over the years, however, the area had become saturated with shopping centers and regional malls, not to mention the Walmarts that sprang up like mushrooms and devastated the mom-and-pop stores. As this trend increased, David and Bob mulled over how they could meet the needs of their tenants and customers, yet still retain South Hills' allure as a community destination environment. In September 2002, they announced a formal plan to de-mall their flagship enterprise to help make it profitable again. Their goal was to ensure the survival of South Hills so it could eventually be passed down to David's grandchildren. At South Hills, de-malling meant consolidating about 30 smaller stores into anywhere from two to five big-box stores and giving these large stores the space that had once been the mall corridors. It also meant the smaller stores would be required to move into another area of the mall, move to the plaza, relocate to another shopping center, or close permanently. For several years prior to this announcement, tenants' leases had included a relocation clause, a standard practice in the industry. Those stores that remained in the mall building had their names prominently displayed on outside signage. [67] Many of the stores were given their own entrances, and management made sure there was ample parking for all. These changes also allowed tenants to have more control over their operating hours. Above all, these changes were meant to benefit South Hills' greatest asset, its loyal customer base.

In February of 2003, David turned 75 years old. He was unfazed by all the tenant shuffling and store expansions and certainly had not slowed down in the least. On a Saturday that April, David was on his way to the Big Lots store on Western Boulevard in Raleigh, when he stopped at a red light. The car in front of him had a bumper sticker that read, "Isaiah 41:10." That scripture paraphrased told the prophet Isaiah and future generations of God's followers not to be afraid because He would strengthen them. [68] David was still pondering the meaning of the scripture when arrived at Big Lots. He heard a lady scream, "Stop him! Stop Him! He stole my purse!" Looking in the direction of the scream, he saw a 50-year-old man, dragging a purse behind him while he ran. The purse had long straps and in the man's haste to get away, it had fallen to the ground. David's instinct to help someone in need immediately kicked in. He left his truck door open and gave chase to the thief. David felt he was running the fastest he had ever run in his life. He chased the man to a retaining wall at the base of a steep embankment leading to a Cook-Out fast food restaurant next door. The man was almost over the wall when David and another man (whom David described as being in his 30's with blond hair and blue eyes) each grabbed one of his ankles and pulled him down. Almost simultaneously and to David's surprise, Wanda Hawley, an Army veteran and employee of Shaw University, raced over to the scene in her vehicle and quickly parked next to where David and the other man were trying to subdue the purse snatcher. Ms. Hawley jumped out of her car to help. David quickly handed her his cell phone, shouting, "Here, call the police!" Ms. Hawley did so and then excitedly called out, "The police are on the way!" David recalled what happened next: "Then he just hauled off and bit the fire out of my left arm. He bit me and wouldn't turn loose." David's prior boxing training came in

---

[67] Megan Jones, "Changes in store for South Hills," *The Cary News*, Thursday, July 31, 2003.
[68] So do not fear, for I am with you; do not be dismayed, for I am your God. I will strengthen you and help you; I will uphold you with my righteous right hand.

handy, and he gave the man a "knuckle sandwich," which forced him to stop biting David. Fortunately, at that point the man was finally subdued.

When the police arrived on the scene, they arrested the purse snatcher and charged him with felony larceny and simple assault. In addition to the police, paramedics responded. They treated David's bite wound and suggested he request his assailant be tested for Hepatitis B, a dangerous bloodborne illness that can cause liver damage. They transported the man to the hospital to be treated for his wounds and then took him to jail.[69]

Marilyn and her daughters first received the call about the incident while attending Debbie's wedding shower. They left as soon as possible to meet David at an urgent care center where a doctor was tending to his bite wound and making sure he was okay.

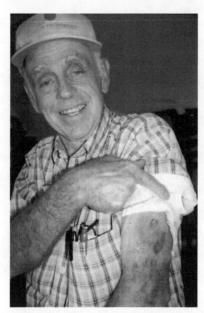

David showing the wound he received when the purse
snatcher he and others stopped at Big Lots bit him.

The doctor asked David when he had last had a tetanus shot. David was not sure. He went into the waiting area and said to Marilyn, "Honey, they want to know when my last tetanus shot was. I can't remember if

---

[69] Ryan Teague Beckwith and Sarah Avery, "Health officials' stance angers victim," *The News and Observer*, April 14, 2008, Sec. B, p. 4.

it was in '44 or '45." Donna said, "Dad, it doesn't matter; you still have to have one!"

The family was amazed to learn how David captured the man. However, when she learned there was no money in the purse, Donna told her father, "Next time, if that happens, ask the lady how much money is in the purse and just give her the money and don't go chasing the man down!"

David took the paramedics' advice and contacted the Wake County Health Department. He asked those officials whether the man could be compelled to be tested for Hepatitis B. The officials replied that since David was not a police officer or another first responder, they were not allowed to require the man to give a sample of his blood. When interviewed by a Raleigh *News and Observer* reporter about the incident Dr. Peter J. Morris, the medical director of the Wake County Human Services Department, declined to discuss the specifics of the case, citing "confidentiality reasons." He said the department's policy was to encourage voluntary testing first, then to seek a court order if anyone— police, paramedic or not—was at risk. That is not what happened in David's case. He asked his son-in-law, Eric, who by then was an Assistant U.S. attorney, to help him contact two county commissioners and the county health director to ask them for permission to have the man tested. They granted his request, but only on the condition that David be tested as well. He recalled the call notifying him of their decision: "The health official called me and wanted to take my blood for testing. I asked why he wanted to take my blood, and he said the man was at a far greater risk of infection than me because he had my blood in his mouth." *The News and Observer* reported this response from Eric: "'They almost turned the whole thing on its head. It was almost as if the victim of the biting was the one who had to be tested more so than the one who did the biting.'" David, who as always was being civic-minded when he helped the purse-snatching victim, said the experience with the health officials left a "bad taste in my mouth," and also said, "Any citizen of North Carolina shouldn't be treated this way. What this is telling people is to not get involved." In the end, the purse snatcher consented to have his blood tested and the matter was put to rest. [70]

---

[70] Ryan Teague Beckwith and Sarah Avery, "Health officials' stance angers victim," The News and Observer, April 14, 2008, Sec. B, p. 4.

A few days after the incident, the lady David had helped called to thank him. While they talked, David asked her if she knew who Ms. Hawley was because he saw the two talking after the police arrived. She told him she had met Ms. Hawley only that day and gave him Ms. Hawley's name and place of employment. Not long afterward, David called Ms. Hawley to thank her for her help. "She told me I was running like h---, and h--- doesn't stand for heaven either," David said. "She said she'd never seen somebody running so fast." But when David asked her if she knew the name of the man who helped him, she said, "There was no other man. You caught him; you pulled him off the wall; you fought him; and you just about broke his jaw. But there was no other man." David said. "I checked that out. There are 275 verses in the Bible about angels. The Lord sent me an angel." He also noted that Psalm 18:33 states: "He makes my feet like the feet of a deer."

In early May, David received a letter from the Wake County District Attorney's office stating that the purse snatcher pled guilty to "Larceny from the Person and Assault (by biting you)." He was sentenced to 24 days in the Wake County Jail with credit for time served and was placed on supervised probation for 24 months.

While the purse snatcher incident may have interrupted Debbie's wedding shower, nothing like it occurred on their wedding day in mid-May 2003 at The Fayetteville Church.

Steve and Debbie were married in May of 2003.

Debbie and her children moved to Fayetteville to be with Steve, and in late May 2004, she gave birth to David and Marilyn's youngest grandchild, Abigail "Abby" Jane Salek. Abby's birth brought the number of Martin granddaughters to eight and the total number of grandchildren to twenty-one.

*Abigail "Abby" Jane Salek, the youngest of the Martins'
21 grandchildren, was born in May 2004.*

CHAPTER 38

Building the Christian Community

Do not withhold good from those to whom it is due,
when it is in your power to act. (Proverbs 3:27 NIV)

Amid all the bustle of David's life, an opportunity for him to donate about 16 acres of land to provide a new site for GRACE Christian School and a church began to emerge. The land, just down the street from South Hills adjacent to South Valley Apartments (which are also owned by the Martin family) is easily accessible to I-40. GRACE Christian School was originally named Mount Olivet Christian School and its administrators started out renting space from Mount Olivet Baptist Church in Raleigh in the early 1980s. The Martin children's involvement with the school began in 1985, when Donna and Eric sent their son, John, to school there. Donna was a substitute teacher and started a fundraising campaign for the school. Eric served on the GRACE Board of Directors for two 2-year terms during the late 1980's and early 1990's. During one of those terms, he was the chairman of the board. His service to the school did not end there. He spearheaded the establishment of the school's athletics program. He also coached the first boys' basketball team, a position he held from 1993-1997. He also coached the girls' basketball team from 2002-2006. Eventually, 16 of the Martin grandchildren attended the school and their parents were actively involved in helping it to succeed. All the Martin daughters were room mothers at some point in time and five of the grandkids graduated from there. As for the school, the administrators had taken advantage of a nominal leasing arrangement with the Mt Olivet Baptist Church, but in 1994, it became a non-profit organization and was renamed Greater Raleigh Area Christian Education, Inc. (GRACE).

In 2001, GRACE school officials were given notice by Mt. Olivet's leadership team that the church intended to terminate their lease. Bob, who also served on the school board, was rounding out his last term as chairman of the board when this occurred. He was especially concerned about the termination of the school's lease. Three of his children were attending GRACE, and he had also planned for his youngest to attend. Moreover, GRACE had recently added a ninth grade, the beginning framework for a future high school. Suddenly, Bob needed to focus on finding a new location for the existing school.

Before he completed his term—with no plan in place or money in the bank to accomplish their goal—the board formed a search committee comprised of five members who were assigned the task of finding a new site. The board members immediately realized that since the school did not provide bus transportation for its students, GRACE would need to lease or construct a building within a zone between U.S. Highway 70 and NC Highway 54. By doing so, they could avoid creating a transportation hardship for the students and their parents, since most of them lived in that area. "So, we searched," he said. "I think we contacted over 90 different churches or facilities. The committee just divvied them up." The group networked with as many people as possible to try to find the right location to rent or buy. "We found out that we were too big for most churches to take us on," Bob said. "We were really struggling."

During their search, the committee members prayed to God, trusting that He knew the path they needed to follow. They also had the conviction that if they were obedient to God's direction, He would take them there. "Whenever the committee filed reports, we praised God for closed doors and open doors, because we just felt like we were really looking for His direction," Bob said. But the committee kept coming up empty-handed. Members found two huge obstacles that encumbered their search in the zones they chose. First was William Umstead State Park, which spans just over 8 square miles between Raleigh, Cary, and Durham. Second was the Raleigh Durham International Airport (RDU). RDU is an 8-mile-long facility located a little over four miles from the town of Morrisville, NC. Things looked so dire for the school that at one strategy session Bob asked the board as well as the school's elementary and upper school principals if the obstacles they encountered might be

God's way of saying GRACE should be absorbed into another school, so that together they would be stronger. Some people who attended the session were taken aback he would even ask the question, but he said it had to be done. Bob was both surprised and heartened by their response. "The school principals—I'll never forget it—said, 'We don't believe God is ready for GRACE Christian School to close just yet!'" With that boost of determination from the principals, the committee kept searching for a solution.

One committee member, who was in the real estate business, did come up with land he thought could be used for the school. The land was ideally situated between West Millbrook Road and NC Highway 50, but the member's efforts were to no avail. Bob explained, "We didn't even have the money in the bank for a down payment. That's how pitiful we were." Fresh out of ideas, Bob told the board members he was unsure if he should be talking about it or not, but he knew of 16 acres of land outside their search area that had been set aside for ministry purposes. He also told the board he had not previously considered it a viable option before because he thought it would be too far for the parents who lived north of the area to travel with their children to school. But Harrison Jones, a search committee member and former board chairman, asked Bob to take the committee to see the land. "So, we drove over to Buck Jones Road. We walked the property, and that's when they asked if I would be willing to talk to Mr. Martin, who owned the land, about GRACE Christian," Bob recalled. He agreed to help and arranged for a meeting between David and the board of directors. When the board met with David, they stressed that if he donated the land to the school, the Christian values taught there would be a form of ministry which would benefit not only the students but the entire community. David was very gracious, but he did not immediately agree to donate the land because he still dreamed of building a church there. Still, the school board members were excited about the possibility. They started communicating to Mount Olivet's leadership team and the school administration that they might have land for their school. Fortunately, when Mt. Olivet's leaders heard the news, they offered to allow the school to continue renting space longer than a year, if needed.

Bob knew that in the eyes of man it appeared the board members had no right to think they could build a school. The school neither owned the land nor had enough collateral for any bank to consider making them a loan. The school board also had not researched whether a foundation or some other legal entity should own the school. Yet, Bob maintained, God had a plan for it to work out.

The way forward came into focus one evening when David and Bob were driving down Buck Jones Road in Raleigh, near what was then a 7-Eleven and later became a Little Sue Mini-Mart. The GRACE board had asked Bob whether the Martins were indeed going to donate the land. He recalled the discussion he had with David about it: "I said, 'Mr. Martin, no disrespect, but our board needs to know. Are you going to give us the land for the school?' He said, 'Bob I made a covenant with God that a church would be on that property, and I just can't break that covenant.' I said, 'So, are you saying that as long as there is a church with the school, you would be okay?' And he said, 'I would consider that.' So, at that point, I knew the only way that site had life for GRACE—and that was my assignment, get GRACE a home—was to get a church."

In the interim, other things were happening that would make the land gift possible. Though David and Bob never actually spoke about it, he allowed Bob to work as the project manager in charge of day-to-day activities associated with building the new school. "It's as if he almost chose to become a partner in developing it, before he signed the deed," Bob said. David's sharing Bob with the school saved thousands of dollars it would have cost to hire someone else. The school also benefited from Bob's knowledge of the inner workings of the board. Additionally, one day David noticed a small, triangular piece of property on the corner near Interstate Highway 40 that used to be an old right-of-way. Immediately he thought that if GRACE officials could purchase this land, it could be added to the land he was already considering donating for their new school. As soon as David saw Bob, he suggested Bob call the North Carolina Department of Transportation (NC DOT) to see if the state would sell it to GRACE. Bob described what happened next: "We called the principal's husband, who at the time was with the NC DOT. One call led to another. The next thing you know, the state said it was a remnant piece of property we could buy. Mr. Martin got his checkbook out, wrote a check for it, then the deed was signed by the governor. That's what you do when you buy from the State of North Carolina; the governor's signature has to hit the deed." The extra land David and Marilyn donated proved to be pivotal when, in late June 2002, Bob went to the City of Raleigh's Planning Department to get the land rezoned. When added to the other two pieces of land the Martins were considering donating, the school had enough land to be recombined instead of subdivided. Thus, the school and a church could be built adjacent to one another and secure financing for their respective projects with separate parcels.

Meanwhile, Bob had to deal with another major issue. The site under consideration for the new school had a huge hill on it. "We had more dirt than we needed," explained Bob, who described it as looking like "an upside-down ice cream cone." At about this time he met a Johnston County grading contractor whose daughter was a student at GRACE. This contractor offered to help with some of the work at the site as long as David intended to donate the land to the school. The contractor also told Bob there were about 100,000 cubic yards of dirt at the site that would need to be removed before construction could begin.

Bob presented this problem to a special joint meeting of GRACE administrators and teachers. One teacher told Bob she could solve the problem by having the dirt hauled to her back yard! He told her he appreciated her willingness to help, but he reminded her there were 100,000 yards of dirt needing to be moved. He recalled how he explained what that much dirt looked like. "It is kind of hard to get your mind around 100,000 yards of dirt, but let me put it this way: You know those big dump trucks that tell you to stay back 200 feet? We basically have 10,000 dump-truck loads of dirt that we need to move." Everyone had a good laugh, and the teacher chimed in that at least they knew where the first two loads could go!

At first Bob was not too concerned about the dirt. He followed instructions from the GRACE board and installed a sign on Buck Jones Road offering fill dirt free of charge to anyone who wanted to haul it away. A few people responded, but they were unwilling to haul away anywhere near the amount of dirt that needed to be moved. One person even offered to buy the land outright when he saw the sign. Bob told the following story about the incident: "Glenn Boyd, the owner of the Crossroads Ford dealership, drove up in a Ford, of all things. He said, 'Hey Bob, why don't you let me buy this property from Mr. Martin. I'll buy you some land down the way there, and we'll put a Ford dealership here. We'll get your GRACE school some land.' I said, 'Mr. Boyd, I'll let Mr. Martin know you said that, but I think this land right here is God's land. I can't even put a water slide on this thing.' I was kind of joking

DAVID L. TIJERINA

with him. It just goes to show that the market wanted this land for commercial purposes. You see how big his dealerships are."

After a good while of not getting any bites on the free dirt offer, Bob was starting to have a bit of a "pity party" about the situation. One Friday, he finally decided he should stop waiting in the office for a phone call and do something to get the ball rolling. He decided to drive around in his truck to see if he could find anyone who advertised a need for dirt. While he was driving along Trailwood Drive, near the NC State Centennial Campus, he came across a huge pile of dirt. Bob thought to himself whoever owned that dirt had the same problem he had. He figured the owner might be able to help him. "It's like the Holy Spirit stopped me and said, 'Bob, if he has the same problem, he might have a solution,'" Bob recounted. "It had to be the Holy Spirit because I'm not that smart." Noting that when people are on a mission for God, they do not have to be bashful about what they do, Bob recalled that he immediately made a U-turn and drove up to a construction trailer parked beside the pile of dirt he had just passed. The trailer was part of another construction site. Once inside, Bob introduced himself to the foreman as a volunteer for GRACE Christian School. While the two talked, Bob jokingly mentioned to the foreman that based on the pile of dirt at the work site, it looked like he had enough. The foreman laughed and said. "You got that right." After exchanging pleasantries, Bob dove right into why he had stopped. He confided in the foreman that he had a similar problem. That comment piqued the foreman's interest. He asked Bob what he meant. Bob recalled how the foreman responded after he was told Bob needed to haul 10,000 truckloads of dirt away from his worksite: "Now that's a lot of dirt! Let me give you the name of a company that deals with big projects."

The foreman gave him the contact information for W.E. Garrison, Inc. in Raleigh. Bob called that company to speak to the project manager, but he was not available. So, Bob left a message stating he was calling on behalf of GRACE Christian School and needed to speak with him about some dirt. That afternoon Hank, the construction manager, returned Bob's call. Hank was eager to hear about the dirt, but first he wanted to know how Bob was affiliated with the school. Bob explained to him that his children attended classes there. Soon their conversation shifted to a discussion about where they both went to church. Then they talked about the dirt on the future site of the school. Bob explained the scope of

188

the project; Hank was stunned. He said, "Bob, I don't think you're going to believe this, but I'll tell you what. When you called this morning, I was in a meeting with all my superintendents. I told them that we were fixing to bid on the site right down here at Highway 64 for the new Hyundai dealer. It was in a hole, and I told them that the bidding was going to be tight and to get out there and start looking for 100,000 yards of dirt. I'm getting chills telling you about it right now. I don't know what the dirt's like. I want to come out early next week, take a sample and see if we can take it off your hands."

Hank went to look at the dirt the next week. His workers took samples to see how compacted it was. When the results came back, he told Bob that on a 1 to 10 scale the dirt was a good 6 or 7! Not long afterward, W.E. Garrison obtained the proper permits to move the dirt. On September 9, 2001, a special worship service was held for GRACE staff, parents, and students to dedicate the land to the glory of God for the future ministry of GRACE Christian School.

Bob continued, "Our grading contractor from Johnston County had a trackhoe on site. One of his employees loaded the trucks with dirt, and the W.E. Garrison drivers would take U.S. 1 South to the Highway 64 exit near McGregor Downs and dump it at a nearby lot. Our contractor donated his employees' time, while the construction company paid the remainder of the costs to haul away the dirt."

While the dirt was being moved, events were falling into place that would allow GRACE to partner with a church, thus fulfilling David's vision for the land. Bob met with several small, medium, and large churches, but none of them quite met the criteria David had set forth. Many of them also could not meet the requirements of the proposed plan for developing the land. Any church that partnered with the school would need to be able to afford the rent for use of the school facilities until a church building could be built a few years later. Though these circumstances might have appeared bleak to most people, David sought to help the GRACE community to stay on track. Kathie Thompson, who served as interim principal of the GRACE Lower Campus (the elementary school) reminisced, "Mr. Martin frequently reminded folks that 'without a vision, the people perish.' He shared that Bible verse, Proverbs 29:18, during a devotional with the GRACE faculty and staff."

One day in the spring of 2001, Emily and Jeff Armandtrout, whose children attended GRACE, informed the school leadership that their church, Hope Community Church, might be interested in partnering with GRACE to develop their project. It appeared to everyone involved that the hand of God was orchestrating events for a partnership to occur. Still unaware of GRACE's need, Hope Community's elders called for a 24-hour-prayer vigil, so members of that church could pray about their growth needs. The prayer vigil began on a Friday at 5 p.m. and was scheduled to end at 5 p.m. the next day. At around 2 a.m. on Saturday night, Mr. Armandtrout handed Pastor Mike Lee, Hope's lead teaching pastor and founder, David's business card. He then told Pastor Lee about GRACE needing a co-developer for the land David was considering donating. The possibility the school and the church could work together was inspiring and intriguing to Pastor Lee!

Hope Community Church was founded by Pastor Lee in 1994, after he and his wife moved to the Triangle area from San Francisco. The church held its kick-off service at East Cary Middle School on Easter Sunday that same year. The congregation met there for a few years but left after the school was remodeled. Their next move was to a commercial building, where the congregation put down roots and stayed for a few years until they outgrew the building. Like GRACE's leaders, Hope's leadership faced difficulties regarding finding affordable land to purchase, and they lacked the funds to construct a building on any land that was found. The news that David wanted to donate land to a church seemed like an answer to the members' prayers. The next week, Pastor Lee called David, and the two met for breakfast to discuss David's vision for the land. "He just really wanted to kind of get to know us, to make sure he knew all about us," Pastor Lee said. As was the case with the GRACE school board, David did not immediately tell Hope's leaders they had a deal, but he did continue to meet Pastor Lee for breakfast occasionally over the next year to discuss the possibility. Finally, one day while they were having breakfast at a Bob Evans restaurant, David informed Pastor Lee that he had decided to give the property to Hope Community Church and GRACE Christian School. Pastor Lee recalled their conversation: "Mr. Martin said that he had had a dream about this property. There was a church on this property, and, he said, there was a pastor speaking at the church. He said, 'It's you. You're the guy. You're the guy in my dream.' I didn't know how to really take that, but when you know Mr. Martin, it's not a surprise at all. And I can still remember where I was sitting in Bob Evans, and this is how Mr. Martin gave us the property. He said, 'Pastor Lee, there's two ways to feed chickens. You can walk into a chicken coop and you can drop a big bag of feed. It'll feed them, but the chickens will scatter. Or you can walk in, and you can drop a few kernels of feed. Those chickens will follow you wherever you go. You know how to feed chickens. I'm giving you guys the property.'"

Meanwhile, David had told the GRACE board members he wanted them to meet with Bobbitt Design Build, a Raleigh-based company. The company uses an integrated building approach that provides architectural design and construction services under one contract. "When we went to see them, they actually showed us a plan for a church," Bob said. "The GRACE school community's reaction to the Bobbitt plan was a little flat. It was a good idea, but it didn't prove to give us the final plan because it was a church plan. The school wasn't included. On the school side, I needed a gym. The plan Bobbitt showed us included only a half-court indoor gym. It wasn't even something that we could hold a game on." The GRACE athletic staff already had to rent space from community centers for their basketball games. The new plan would leave them in the same predicament.

Bobbitt went back to the drawing board and presented a new plan to the GRACE school community. The new plan included a full-sized gym, which satisfied the school's stakeholders. In the meantime, the land had been graded, a retaining wall was built, ground utilities were laid, and the Hope Community Church leadership team had toured the site. Since David had yet to sign the two land parcels over to the school or the church, Bob and the GRACE board were beginning to wonder if he really intended to donate the land. Things finally came to a head when Bob and GRACE school representatives met to discuss the plans for the school with an official from the City of Raleigh Planning Department. As they were about to look at the plans, the official asked for the deed to the property. Bob informed her that the school did not have one. She said if the school board intended to get a building permit, she would need to see a deed that proved GRACE owned the land. Next, in what Bob called a "defining moment," he approached his in-laws and told them the school was ready to get its building permit. David told him to go ahead and get his permit. Bob responded, "Well, Mr. Martin, um, the City won't give us the permit until we have the deed." "Fortunately, we had identified Hope," Bob recalled. "Hope had an attorney that was helping them to form an agreement with GRACE Christian School, and Mr. and Mrs. Martin realized that it was time for the ink to hit the paper."

The Martins had their attorney draw up a separate document entitled, "Declaration of Easements, Covenants and Restrictions," which spelled out the Martins' conditions for donating the land to each entity and their wishes for how the two organizations would cooperate going forward. One of the conditions outlined in this document was that Hope Community Church affiliate with the Southern Baptist Convention. Representatives from both organizations signed their respective deeds, as well as the accompanying declaration, on August 29, 2002. The monetary value of the Martins' land donation was between $3.5 and $4 million. Under the terms of their agreement, Bob added, Hope went ahead and paid half of the development costs, including landscaping, parking lots, etc., allowing the school building to be constructed first and its leaders went on faith that construction of their church building would soon follow.

With much of the normal site preparation work already complete, GRACE was issued a permit to begin construction on its 52,000 square-foot building on September 11, 2002. "Early in the building process, each class in our school chose a significant scripture verse that would reflect the mission of our school," Ms. Thompson related. "Once the concrete foundation was poured for the new building, we brought a student representative from each class over to the new campus to literally write the scripture verses on the foundation of the school building. So, our school is both figuratively and physically built on God's Word!" Work on the school was completed and a certificate of occupancy issued on August 29, 2003, less than one year from the day the permit was issued, a phenomenal pace for a project of that size! A dedication service was held in the school gym just before classes began.

*After much prayer and work, Grace Christian
School was completed in August of 2003.*

During the building's inaugural year, the 2003-2004 school year, the student population was just under 300 students. The students selected "Blueprints" as the theme for their yearbook and dedicated it to their benefactors, David and Marilyn Martin. At the time of this book's publication, there are almost 800 students enrolled at GRACE. "The vision given to Mr. Martin and to our school leaders is being lived out in the lives of our alumni, students, faculty and staff," Ms. Thompson said. "We were blessed to receive the generous gift of land on Buck Jones Road. The impact of that gift continues to impact the world for Christ!"

In October 2003, Hope Community Church began meeting in the GRACE school gym. The congregation would worship there for the next two years, paying a substantial amount of rent to help the school gain a firm financial footing. The Hope congregation numbered 1,000 members when they started holding services at GRACE.

Construction of the Hope Community Church campus began
in September 2004 and was completed in January 2006.

When construction began on their 92,000-square-foot building in September 2004, the church leadership was not sure how they were going to pay for it. Fortunately, by the time construction was complete in January 2006, church membership had increased to 3,000, and the members could afford to pay for the building and its upkeep.

In May 2007, GRACE and Hope partnered again to purchase the 56,000-square-foot former Crossroads Ford dealership adjacent to what was then the K&S Cafeteria at South Hills. David's friend and the owner of the property, Glenn Boyd, first offered the property to him. However, David knew that GRACE and Hope were interested and needed more space. As quoted in a *News and Observer* article later that year, David explained, "I backed off. I wouldn't dare go against God's folks. He might strike me down."[71] Plans were made for GRACE to hold high school classes there during the week and Hope to hold its youth program there on weekends. Hope ended up not needing the building as much as anticipated and sold it to GRACE in August 2016. The building was remodeled and has become the GRACE Upper Campus, housing grades 9-12.

Hope has grown at a phenomenal rate over the past 12 years, purchasing several additional properties and merging with two other

---

[71] "Overheard," *The News and Observer*, July 8, 2007, Sec. A, Page 25, Col. 1.

churches. The church now has an average attendance of approximately 15,000 worshippers among five campuses. Their first and largest campus is the site donated by the Martins at 821 Buck Jones Rd. in west Raleigh. Hope now also has a location in South Raleigh, the Ship of Zion Church and Outreach Ministries. In addition, Hope also operates campuses in Morrisville and at their newest facility in Apex. Last, but not least, Hope's outreach extends to their international campus in Port Au Prince, Haiti. "The growth of the church never would have happened without Mr. Martin giving us this piece of property," Pastor Lee said. He further related that Mr. Martin has sent quite a few Baptist ministers to visit Hope to learn how they can help their own churches grow at the rate Hope has grown.

In the nearly 15 years the two organizations have shared the land, except for an occasional scheduling issue, they have had practically no conflict. They also share parking spaces when one of them is holding a special event. David also allows church members to park at South Hills and catch Hope's shuttle from the GRACE Upper Campus next door. "To me, that's probably the miracle of this situation—that two Christian organizations can sit on the same property and not fight," Pastor Lee said. "I feel like we were able to see Mr. Martin's dream become a reality." Not only that, he added, but the church has also helped many people whose lives were shipwrecked before they dedicated them to God. He gave examples of two such people in the interview for this book. One such person is a young woman who was working as a stripper at a Raleigh night club when her parents persuaded her to come with them to church. After hearing the message of Jesus, she was baptized. To help make her exit from her previous lifestyle permanent, the church offered her a job as a secretary so she could obtain work skills and not be tempted to go back to her former employment. At the time of the writing of this book, she has been employed by the church for nearly 15 years. Still another person is a young man who was living in Los Angeles and was working as an actor and director in the porn film industry. He had participated in the production of over 600 pornographic movies. He finally became so frustrated with himself and sick of that industry that he moved back to North Carolina. Once in the area, he began attending services at Hope Community Church. Recently, he dedicated his life to God. "His life has changed radically," Pastor Lee said. Pastor Lee added that he could cite example after example of people whose lives have been radically changed when they encountered and received the Gospel at Hope Community Church.

He added that Hope Community Church is geared toward reaching out to the community. "Our statement of faith is actually Baptist, because I grew up Baptist, but we were hesitant to name it a Baptist church because there's a million different kinds of Baptists and there's stereotypes that go with Baptists just like there are stereotypes that go with any denomination," Pastor Lee said. "Mr. Martin knew that our target was not reaching other Baptists. It was reaching people who weren't Christians. We felt like just having the word Baptist on it might hinder some people who aren't Christians from coming." The church does work with the Southern Baptist Convention and is a general cooperating member church. A cooperating member church makes a one-time donation every year to the convention. "We are not voting members, and we don't have any say in the politics of the convention," Pastor Lee continued. "We can take advantage of Baptist Men for hurricane relief and things like that." He added the interesting thing is that Hope is nothing like a church he believes Mr. Martin would want to join. "We have a couple of thousand college kids here every Sunday, most of them from NC State, Campbell, and Meredith," he said. "That's kind of the generation it appeals to, but Mr. Martin understands that to reach people for the Gospel sometimes things need to be different. So, I think for his ability to see outside of what would be his preference, to the bigger picture of people coming to Christ, it speaks to his maturity in a way that you rarely see in our culture today." Pastor Lee added that even though David is not an ordained minister, he could not think of many people who have given as much thought to advancing the Kingdom of God as David does.

Looking back on the time they devoted to securing the site for the school and the church, Bob believes God allowed David to maximize his stewardship of the land. Shared use between the two organizations allowed the property to be used seven days a week as opposed to weekends only, as would have happened with a church alone. As often happens when people serve and give to others unselfishly, Bob and David benefited, too. Bob continued, "I got a great education on site development, building development, and all sorts of things that perhaps I wouldn't have had exposure to. So, it's as if I was sent off to school to learn more about site planning and building."

The land gift also keeps paying non-monetary dividends for David. He recently learned that his longtime friend George King—who he met and grew close to at First Baptist Church in Cary in the 1950s—has two grandchildren enrolled at GRACE, including granddaughter Micah, the 2017 Homecoming Queen! In an interview for this book, Mr. King added this about David: "If for no other reason, if his legacy is only associated with Hope and the school and what it has meant for so many Christian families, it can't be measured."

CHAPTER 39

Felling Trees

For there is a proper time and procedure for
every matter, though a person may be weighed
down by misery. (Ecclesiastes 8:6 NIV)

Besides working with their grandfather as children, some of David's grandsons have worked for him during summer vacations or when they were on college breaks. A few have worked for him after college as well. His grandson, John, worked for him around 2005 or 2006. Whether a person worked full-time for Martin Properties or as a subcontractor in the field for David, he or she was in for vigorous work, John said. "We would have to operate at Granddaddy's pace and work 'till dark thirty,' almost on a rural farm time clock—all day long. There wasn't a clock to punch out on. When five o'clock rolled around and we were ready to go home, if we saw that little red truck or that blue Dodge he used to drive, oh, man, we'd make a collective groan at the job site. We knew then we weren't going home yet. Then he'd walk up and be ready to put a door in, dig a ditch, or whatever else he wanted done." In fact, it was about the time John started to work for his grandfather as an adult that David began to have what John saw as an obsession for cutting down trees. However, this "obsession" was well-founded.

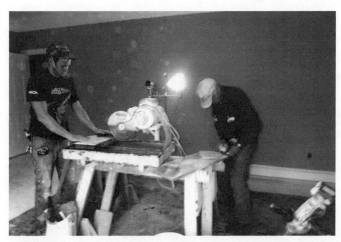

During the time John (left) worked for his grandfather (right) they did not just fell trees; they also built a new home for the Martins.

David had seen first-hand numerous instances in which trees had fallen onto houses, causing significant damage. In one instance, a large branch had fallen through the roof of one of his apartments, impaling itself in a tenant's bed. Fortunately, the tenant was not in the bed! John said, "He would rant and rail about how a hurricane would knock those trees down, how the roots were too shallow, or how they would leave a daggering branch after one blew through that could hurt someone."

One of David's famous tree felling exercises occurred at University Apartments while John was working for his grandfather: The property has always had an abundance of old pines, but back then, there were 78 more, John said. At the time, David rented a Sunbelt boom truck and had one of his employees cut off the top of each tree. After the top was removed, he would have another worker knock the rest of it down with a backhoe. "He just got on a tear," John said. "It was weeks and weeks of tree cutting. He had me sitting there with a stump grinder attached to my Silverado truck. We took down tree after tree. Those things fell, and it was like the time of the dinosaurs out there. If people were to walk the sidewalks at the apartments, they'd see where those trees fell and split the sidewalks." John added that when he went home at night he'd jokingly tell his wife that when he blew his nose an entire oak tree and sweet gum tree had come out! "I remember we ground so many trees that

Sunbelt had to come out and replace the blade on the stump grinder," he said. "I mean it was like a full-scale operation."

A tree David's crew felled near one lady's house did not land where intended. The bushy end of the tree landed on her house. "She came out screaming," John said. "She had a towel wrapped around her head because she had been in the shower when the tree hit. While she was throwing her hands up, her finger mistakenly grabbed that towel and she swatted it towards my granddaddy," John said. "I remember him grabbing it while she was just chewing him out. He politely folded it, then handed it to her! That lady sure was upset that day. She also claimed to be a relative of then Senator John Edwards." When she calmed down a bit, John said, his grandfather apologized to her. He also made sure any damage to her home was repaired.

Not long after that incident, City of Raleigh zoning enforcement officials learned David was cutting down the trees. Raleigh has strict regulations governing tree removal so David was issued a citation stating that he would be fined $500 a day for each additional tree he cut down. David immediately called Bob, who in turn began researching the city code governing tree removal on private property. His research revealed that a property owner was not required to obtain a permit if their land was less than three acres in size. Bob also discovered that University Apartments is comprised of several pieces of land each *under* three acres in size. David saw no need to inform the City of Raleigh about its own code, so when he learned he was not in violation, he had his crew resume felling trees. When city officials arrived to tell him to cease his tree removal, David showed them the proof he was within his rights to cut them down. John recalled, "So it was almost like he said, 'I know what I can do and I'm going to keep doing it until they come out here. Then I'm going to poke them with their own ordinance and show them I have a right to cut my trees down.'"

CHAPTER 40

Back at Triangle Forest

Therefore everyone who hears these words of mine and puts them into practice is like a wise man who built his house on the rock. The rain came down, the streams rose, and the winds blew and beat against that house; yet it did not fall, because it had its foundation on the rock. (Matthew 7:24-25 NIV)

In 2005, David and Marilyn decided they wanted to live closer to their children and made plans to construct a new home on West Marilyn Circle. David, with help from his family, his employees, his regular contractors, and several sub-contractors called in especially for the job, built a beautiful, spacious residence right across the street from two of his daughters and just down the street from two others.

(From left to right) Parker, Martin, Kristen and John, on the truck, and two Martin Properties employees load the front door to the Martins' home.

David was personally involved in the entire process from the grading of the land until the finishing touches were added. Donna remembers that before the walls were painted her father let the family write their favorite Scriptures on the walls of the new home.

The Martins' granddaughter, Kristen, writes a scripture on one of the walls of her grandparents' home in Triangle Forest before it was completed.

She added he also bought a cordless drill for each of his 21 grandchildren so they could help him in the construction of the house.

As has always been the case wherever David and Marilyn lived, their home quickly became the central meeting place for their children, grandchildren and their families. One family gathering that began the first summer in their new home and has continued each summer is Monday Pizza Night. On those evenings, Marilyn buys the pizzas and each family unit that attends provides a salad or dessert for the gathering. Afterward, the entire extended family sits on the front porch so David's son-in law Eric can ask the question of the week. Everyone present who is able shares their viewpoint on the question. "The question of the week has really helped my kids a lot," David's daughter Diane said. "It's helped them with expressing their conservative views and taught them how to defend themselves, whatever the topic is—politics or religion or whatever." One summer each family was given a copy of the Dale Carnegie book, *How to Win Friends and Influence People,* which David credits with being instrumental in helping him succeed in his business pursuits. Each family member was asked to read a chapter each week to be prepared for the group discussion. Discussing this book positively changed the lives of several of the Martin grandchildren.

David's son-in-law Will Stephenson said the establishment of the Monday Pizza Night tradition represents only one of the changes David has made in his life to make more time for family over the past decade. "Ten years ago, he would sit right here and tell you you're crazy to own a boat. You shouldn't own a boat. It's a waste of time and it's a waste of money," Will said. "Now, I'm not going to tell you he'd go out on my boat to this day. But he doesn't make those comments anymore. I think he's realizing that family time can be important. We've tried to help him see that. We're doing it different than the way he did it." Will added that about a year ago David, Jr. started going to his parents' house every Saturday night so they can go out to eat pizza. "I think it's healthy for them to have that bonding time," Will said.

CHAPTER 41

Holding on to a Landmark

*Get rid of all bitterness, rage and anger, brawling and
slander, along with every form of malice. Be kind and
compassionate to one another, forgiving each other, just
as in Christ God forgave you. (Ephesians 4:31-32 NIV)*

In December 2007, the Town of Cary filed a lawsuit against South Hills
Shopping Center, Inc. and its president, David Martin, concerning the
South Hills pole sign that had marked the mall's location since 1972.
Located in front of the NC License & Title office, the sign was situated
a bit further north on the property than the current monument sign.
It was an illuminated marquee-type sign with changeable copy and
was considered a local landmark. Town officials told the *Cary News*
the pole sign with its red changeable letters and gray poles violated the
town's recently enacted sign ordinance. David was already unhappy
about the ordinance because he suspected one of the reasons behind
it was the disapproval in some quarters of the conservative messages
he posted on it. Since the sign was initially approved back when South
Hills was in the City of Raleigh—before a land swap between the two
municipalities—David felt the Town of Cary's authority in this matter
should be limited. [72]

A total of 19 businesses were affected by the new sign ordinance
and were required to remove their existing signs. Bob felt the Town of
Cary Planning Board did a poor job of notifying these owners of the

---

[72] Sadia Latifi. "South Hills placard signs off," *The Cary News*. Sunday, February
212, 2010. Page 1 A.

implications of the new requirements. "Apparently, there was a meeting," Bob said. "At the meeting, it was determined that it would be fair to amortize the signs, or retire them after a certain period, but none of the people that were impacted were invited to come out and speak out against it. So, we inherited this communication that said, by the way, you're one of 19 pole owners. We want your sign to be retired in two to three years, and you have to follow the new rules. You're not grandfathered forever. We're going to give you a grace period, but it will end." The new rules called for more uniform signs, which the board believed would make Cary a more attractive town, Bob said.

Though Bob did not necessarily agree with the way the Town's ordinance had been implemented, some of the messages David displayed on the South Hills marquee had been the subject of much debate between the two men. Bob sometimes succeeded in persuading David not to display some of the proposed messages, fearing they might offend his tenants and customers, thereby losing business for the mall. Sometimes Bob's view did not prevail and the message David intended was displayed anyway.

David felt that not only was the ordinance enacted for political reasons, but also that the process by which it was enacted was flawed. He refused to take the sign down. Other citizens had complied with the Town's request, and Cary officials felt that if they let David keep his sign up, they would be accused of showing favoritism. The impasse would continue for nearly two and a half years, with the Town charging a $500 fine for each day it was left standing.

During the impasse, life went on for David. In January 2008, when he was almost 80 years old, he showed no signs of slowing down. *The News and Observer* interviewed him and several other people who had come of age during the Great Depression for an article featuring persons over age 75 who were still in the workforce. David observed that retirement often leaves people without a purpose. He also said, "My only retirement plan is to retire to bed each night, so the Lord can restore my strength, and I can get up and do it again the next day."[73]

---

[73] Thomas Goldsmith, Retire at 75? Not these folks," *The News and Observer*, pg. 1B and 4B.

David next to a sign at South Hills
that echoes his sentiment about retirement.

In fact, David was inspired by his good friend, Mabel Riggan, who lived to be 106 years old. When she asked him, "David, what do you plan to do when you get to be my age?" he replied, "I *might* cut back to 40 hours a week!"

Another good friend of David's, Senator Jesse Helms, passed away on July 4th, 2008. When he learned of the senator's death, David displayed a message on the South Hills marquee that read: "Jesse Helms, 1921-2008, An American Hero."

David displayed a message on the South Hills Marquee that
honored Sen. Jesse Helms when he died in 2008.

A photo of this sign appeared in a special four-page pull-out section of *The News and Observer* the following day. When David was asked about his tribute to the late senator, David explained that Helms had helped him and also noted, "He's responsible for the Iron Curtain falling." David's response was in recognition of Helms's service on the Senate Foreign Relations Committee, including his chairmanship from 1995-2001. Helms, through his work on this committee, helped Secretary of State Madeline Albright and President Ronald Reagan influence events leading to the dismantling of the Soviet Union.

At Senator Helms's funeral, David's grandson, John, saw just how deeply connected his grandfather was with the older generation of North Carolina Republican politicians. When David entered the church, he walked straight to the front and loudly said, "Paging Russell Capps!" John recalled that many of the politicians who attended the funeral said, 'Hey, David!' in response. "Granddaddy was definitely connected to the older prominent political figures in North Carolina," John said. He also noted that his grandfather seemed unconcerned that Delaware Senator Joe Biden, who later became Vice-President, and South Dakota Senator Tom Daschle, the former U.S Senate majority leader, were among other national figures on the front row as David bellowed his greeting to Representative Capps.

David was known to the older political establishment in Raleigh because he had been an enthusiastic supporter of their causes. He also loved attending and donating to candidates at political fundraisers, and, besides supporting Sen. Helms over the years, he has also supported many other conservative politicians. Of course, stories about his battles with the Town of Cary and other government agencies did not escape their attention either.

The impasse between David and the Town of Cary regarding the South Hills pole sign finally ended in February 2010. Bob had taken the role of mediator between his father-in-law and Town officials. "We tried all sorts of things," he said. "We worked with different members of the council; we worked with their staffs; and, finally, we worked out a compromise with the Town. That compromise meant taking the sign down and building one that complied with the ordinance." Under the agreement, if David complied with the Town's demands by May 31, 2010, and removed the sign, town officials promised to waive the $484,850 in fines he had accrued. The Town also allowed David to build the replacement sign close to the fence separating the South Hills property from U.S. #1. The Town normally did not allow signs to be erected in that corridor. These concessions were definite wins for Martin Properties. Conversely, Town officials succeeded in their goal of requiring David to have the new sign built several feet higher than the pole sign it replaced and to use brick comprised of at least 70 percent material which matched the surrounding buildings. The following year, when the new monument sign was first completed, the sign ordinance limited the display of the words "South Hills" to only two sides of the three-sided structure. This ordinance was later liberalized enabling South Hills and other Cary business owners with similar signs to display their business name on all sides of their signs.

After the compromise was reached, David told a reporter from *The Cary News* that he wanted to get along with the Town of Cary and to work with town leaders for the betterment of the community. The reporter noted that his response was a "marked shift in tone" for a man who—though he was a staple in the town's Christian community and a well-regarded developer—had declared the previous August he would not take his sign down no matter how high the fine. Now David maintained he made that comment as a red-blooded American who just wanted to stand up for what was right. He also told the reporter he

The day the marquee was removed David's family and employees made an event of it.

wanted to give Bob and the Town credit because they had gotten an old, stubborn man to change. David added that at age 82 he was at a point in his life where it was more important to build relationships than anything else. The sign did not get thrown away, though.[74]

David kept it, and, with a gleam his eye, told the reporter he planned

[74] Sadia Latifi. "South Hills placard signs off", *The Cary News*. Sunday, February 212, 2010. Page 1 A.

to do something 'real newsworthy' with it. Before David could put any plan into action, however, his family and employees, who knew he was not happy about having to take down his sign, decided to turn the day it was lowered into a special promotional event. "We had T-shirts. The family came out. We sold hot dogs at 1972 prices, as in the year South Hills was built. We also had a radio remote hooked up so Mr. Martin could move the crane that took it down," Bob recalled.

His family and Martin Properties staff planned to have David fly in on a helicopter for the event, but a forecast for bad weather quashed this plan. That was just fine with David because he later admitted he had been a little squeamish about flying in a helicopter anyway. Bob reminisced, "We had a stage set up. When the crane was supposed to lift the sign and set it on a trailer to haul it away, he didn't have the heart to say take it down. So, he had me say. 'Take it down.' Kind of like the T.V. show, where they said, 'Move that Bus.' We built the other sign later that year."

Bob thought he and David were through dealing with the whole sign issue until one weekend in December 2010, when Bob got a call from David's attorney. The attorney had just finished having a telephone conversation with the Town's planning director. That official informed the attorney that the sign David agreed would never again be displayed in Cary was set up on a trailer on South Hills property along U.S. Highway 1 displaying the message: "Jesus is the Reason for the Season, God Bless America." "He had rigged that up by himself on a weekend," Bob said. "He parked it right by the exit ramp and was kind of being a little bit of a free-spirit."

Bob immediately called his father-in-law. David told him he had displayed the sign because he wanted to celebrate Christmas! Bob told him that the Town's planning director had seen it and was displeased that David had apparently reneged on their agreement. Bob also reminded David they had buried the hatchet with the Town officials, who had forgiven the large fine. David assured Bob that he would move it. Thinking the sign was on its way back into storage, Bob informed the attorney the matter was settled. However, David was not through yet! He moved it just outside the Cary town limits to a vacant lot owned by the Martin Family in Apex. "It was almost as if he was saying to Cary, 'OK, I got it, you don't want it in your jurisdiction. That's fine; I've got other land in other districts.' He was just again wanting to share that message: 'Jesus is the reason for the season, God bless America.'"

It was not long before Bob received a call from the Apex planning director, who told him a permit was required to display the sign. David either had to get one or have the sign removed. Bob approached David again and received the same assurance the former marquee would be moved. To Bob's disbelief, David did indeed move the sign—this time to land he owned just inside the Raleigh city limits. Bob said it was almost like David was a renegade, trying to display his sign anywhere he could. Apparently, the area planning directors must have been talking to each other. Bob received a similar call from the City of Raleigh—again about David needing a permit to display the sign. Raleigh's planning director showed a little more understanding, though, and allowed David to keep the sign up until after Christmas.

Finally, the old South Hills marquee was moved to a storage facility where it remained for over a year. One day, David told Bob he would like to enter the sign in the Cary Christmas Parade. Because of David's history of conflict with the Town, Bob asked him if he was sure he wanted the sign in the parade. David replied, "yes" and directed Bob to ask the Cary Town officials for permission to do so. Bob contacted Cary Town Manager Ben Shivar and asked for permission to have the sign in the parade. Bob and Mr. Shivar had a civil discussion about David's request, but Mr. Shivar reminded Bob that the Cary Jaycees, not the Town, sponsored the parade. Mr. Shivar had no problem with the sign being in the parade if the Jaycees did not. David was grateful to the Jaycees and, with one exception, his sign has appeared in the Cary Christmas Parade every year since.

CHAPTER 42

A Grandson's Hero

*Bear with each other and forgive one another if any
of you has a grievance against someone. Forgive as
the Lord forgave you. (Colossians 3:13 NIV)*

Whether he consciously cultivated it or was born with it, a "sixth sense" that David has displayed throughout his adult life enables him to judge which people need his help the most and when these folks need him to spend time with them. One of these people was David's grandson, Parker Stephenson. Following in the footsteps of his older brothers and cousins, Parker grew up in a loving and caring home environment. His parents taught him the difference between right and wrong and regularly took him to church. As early as age six he also had the opportunity to spend time with his grandfather. During their time together, David reinforced the spiritual and life lessons that Will and Diane were already teaching Parker. But everyone has to travel their own path in life, whether smooth or bumpy. Parker, who turned 26 in 2017, was no different.

In his late teens and early twenties Parker began to make poor decisions. In early 2013, he lost his driving license, but was allowed to drive to and from work.

Despite that setback good things were still happening in Parker's life. In June 2013, he obtained his first career-level position as a salesman with a Chevrolet dealership in Fuquay-Varina, NC. He did well there and attributed his success to advice his grandfather had given him. After Parker had shown a dislike for working in the family business, David pointed out that Parker's gifts would be better suited to a sales position. Parker had never forgotten the stories his grandfather told him about his experiences selling cars at the Lincoln-Mercury dealership. When it came time to pick a sales career, Parker chose auto sales. He added that after he started working there, David called him to see how things were going. When he heard how well Parker was doing, David was not in the least bit surprised!

Later in 2013, due to more poor choices, Parker's license was suspended. However, in consideration of his excellent sales performance, his supervisors at the Chevy dealership allowed him to keep his job so long as he had transportation to and from work.

At that point, Parker was in a dark place and felt he was slipping into depression. He was dismayed about the consequences of his actions and beating himself up for making such poor decisions. That is when his grandfather stepped in, being there for him when no one else was. David drove the 21 miles or so to Parker's job and took him out to lunch. During their time together, David encouraged Parker by telling him how much he cared for him, believed in him, and wanted to see him succeed. "I expected him to be upset at me and to be really disappointed in me for bringing that kind of negative attention on our family, but he did the total opposite," Parker said. "He reached out his arms and hugged me and ultimately said he loved me."

Without a license it was difficult for Parker to get to and from work. Eventually, he was forced to quit his job at the Chevy dealership. The loss of his income meant he could neither afford the rent for his apartment nor make his monthly truck payments. Consequently, he lost them both. Amid all this misfortune, the silver lining for Parker was his grandfather hiring him to work for Martin Properties. From September 2014 until June of 2015, grandfather and grandson worked side by side. David drove, of course. Parker was even allowed to sit in on business meetings. He added that two of the most important things he learned from his grandfather were how to treat people fairly and how to use the power of persuasion to influence people and events for the better.

During the time he worked for his grandfather, Parker hired a good lawyer to handle his legal matters. In addition to everything else he did to help his grandson, David also kept up with Parker's court dates. David knew the date when his grandson would learn the final disposition of his case, including whether he would lose his license for the next four years. After 22 months of waiting, Parker was found not guilty and immediately regained his driving privileges. When Parker learned the verdict, the first person he called was David. "When I called my grandfather that morning and told him that the case was dismissed and that I was going to be able to pick up the pieces and move on in my life, it was crazy because he already knew what the outcome would be." Looking back on the episode, Parker believed his grandfather's attitude must have been a product of his deep Christian faith. Parker was amazed that David was at peace even before the verdict was rendered. While Parker was still in shock over the sudden happy turn of events, David praised God when he heard the good news. He told Parker he had been given "another chance at life!" "One day, when he is no longer here, I will always remember that," Parker said. "I will always remember the person that he was and the fact that he showed so much grace when he didn't have to."

Unfortunately, Parker passed away on May 30, 2018. After his death, the family found an e-mail he had sent to a friend. In it Parker said he wanted to be remembered like his grandfather will be remembered: as a man of God and as a family man. He noted that while David had become successful, he always put Jesus first and himself last. He added that his grandfather never had to tell him what to do but rather showed him what to do through the life he lived. "He always trusts God and is the definition of a servant," Parker wrote. Besides that, he said his grandfather was slow to anger, didn't judge, thought before he spoke and, despite his advanced age and the illnesses that come with it, he didn't sweat the small things and had made the most he could out of life.

Parker is pictured with his son Brantley and wife
Celeste on a snowy day in Cary, NC.

CHAPTER 43

The Hometown Spirit Award

A good name is more desirable than great riches; to be esteemed is better than silver or gold. (Proverbs 22:1 NIV)

True honor is the honor that is bestowed on a person by his peers. Nominated by his good friends, Joe and Edna Sturdivant and Margie McLawhorn, David, at age 86, was awarded the Hometown Spirit Award by the Town of Cary on November 20, 2014!

David and Marilyn in November 2014, when he was presented the Cary Hometown Spirit Award.

This annual award recognizes community-minded citizens who enhance the quality of life in the Town of Cary by preserving, promoting, and carrying out small-town community values and traits. The award was presented to David at a Town Council meeting with his family, friends, and various city dignitaries in attendance.

The Town Clerk's administrative assistant, Ginny Johnson, summarized David's contribution to Cary in a press release that was distributed to news organizations at the time. "Be it chicken coops or commercial centers, David's thumbprint is leaving a lasting impression on Cary, one our community is so grateful to receive. His community involvement is a model for other citizens as we all work together to keep Cary one of the greatest places to live, work and raise a family."

The press release also noted that David was known to have coined the phrase, "The only place you can go better than Cary is heaven."

CHAPTER 44

Developing a Leader

The student is not above the teacher, but everyone who is
fully trained will be like their teacher. (Luke 6:40 NIV)

David's grandson Martin is so far the only one of his and Marilyn's grandchildren who has chosen to make working for the family business a career. "Martin," whose full name is David Martin Stephenson, earned his B.S. degree in Business Management with a minor in Human Resources from Guilford College, Greensboro, NC, in 2011. After graduation, he worked for a landscaping company for several years and also considered pursuing a career in law enforcement. Eventually, he decided to work for his grandfather's company.

Like his namesake, Martin loves to work, and, in the autumn of 2015, he was hired as the maintenance services manager at Martin Properties. Martin enjoys working for his grandfather, and he wants to see the company remain viable in the future. "I want to help continue what Granddaddy started," Martin said.

Martin would like to emulate his Uncle Bob in striving for self-improvement, so he can better help the

Martin Stephenson. "I want to help continue this business so it's there for the generations of family to come."

company grow. Since joining the company, Bob has earned his Certified Property Manager (CPM®) designation from the Institute of Real Estate Management (IREM) and Certified Shopping Center Manager (CSM) designation from the International Council of Shopping Centers (ICSC). Martin hopes, like Bob, to progress in his career and expand his role at Martin Properties.

Martin is in a unique position. Not only can he get advice about career progression from his uncle, but he can also get direct grooming from the founder of Martin Properties, his grandfather. Martin realizes that his grandfather wants to pass on all the lessons he has learned on his journey to success. He is also teaching Martin how to spot land with development potential and how to develop the land he purchases. Working with his grandfather can also be fun, Martin related. "We'll be out and about, and he will say, 'This is David Martin, too, and he's my boss!' While attending meetings with his grandfather or working independently, Martin has noticed that he is treated with more respect when he uses his given name. Whether he is the only one of David's grandchildren to commit to a career within the family business remains to be seen, but for now Martin is reaping the benefits of working for the enterprise.

CHAPTER 45

Putting His House in Order

*A good person leaves an inheritance for their
children's children, but a sinner's wealth is stored
up for the righteous. (Proverbs 13:22 NIV)*

In August 2013, David and Marilyn's oldest grandson presented them
with their first great-grandchild, Savannah. Six weeks later, in October,
their second great-grandchild, Mason, was born. Then in January 2014,
granddaughter Kristen gave birth to Kinsey Marilyn. By the end of 2014,
David had five great-grandchildren with the additions of Brantley and
Emma. Savannah's sister, Magnolia, brought in 2016, and Kinsey's sister,
Carli, closed out 2016. Dotty's first grandchild, Henry, was born in 2017,
and Mason's little sister, Della, was born in early 2018. By the end of 2018,
two more great-grandchildren, Augie and Ryleigh, had joined the family!

In mid-2016, David's children began to urge him to do some
estate planning. He had already established a trust for them and his
grandchildren and transferred some of his property into it but had
not done much more than that. Such matters were just not part of his
mindset. Buttressed by his strong faith in God's ability to cure any
sickness or disease, as well as his extraordinary capacity to handle pain,
he is not a man who dwells on the idea of his own death. Therefore,
he had not given serious consideration to estate planning. After many
discussions with his family, he placed a portion of his various assets into
a new company called Greater South Hills, LLC. On Christmas Day, he
surprised his children by joyfully giving each of them the gift of a stake
in the company!

That same year, Bob's title changed to General Property Manager of Martin Properties. He explained that, in this role, he is now responsible for the day-to-day functioning of both the commercial and the residential divisions. Previously, he had oversight of only the commercial division. With oversight of both divisions, the thought was that he could help relieve the overlapping of work orders and ensure proper accounting procedures between the two entities.

Joyful times can sometimes be followed by difficult ones and the accompanying hard decisions. David's vision had begun to weaken significantly in 2016 to the point that his doctor advised him he should no longer drive. Hearing the doctor's recommendation was difficult for David. He was still doing things in his late 80's that many men stop doing in their 70's or sooner. He was accustomed to driving himself to his various meetings, to church, to visit people, and to job sites at will. Also taking into consideration the fact that David, among his other capabilities, could still climb a ladder to the top of a roof, the thought of having to stop driving was not one he relished. It was a struggle for him, but eventually, in April 2017, he decided to comply with the doctor's order. He did not slow down though. With the aid of his family and his employees, who drive him to and from various appointments and worksites, he maintains a busy six-day work week, He can be found at South Hills, University Apartments, South Valley Apartments, or other properties as needed.

David was going along with life as usual when on June 27, 2017, after being ill for about a week, he was admitted to Rex Hospital in Raleigh. To his shock, he learned he had stage-four prostate cancer. His prostate-specific antigen level (PSA) was 765. According to the website WebMd, a PSA level of only 4.0 can indicate prostate cancer!

Many of David's family and friends came to see him while he was in the hospital, bringing him cards and flowers. They shared their memories with him and quite a few recounted how he helped them in some way. Due to his advanced age, David was not eligible for chemotherapy or radiation therapy, so his doctor prescribed hormone therapy, and he was discharged from the hospital after nine days. The family hired a home-health agency to assist David during his recovery.

Before long, David was out and about checking on several houses he was remodeling and working at his office at South Hills. At first, he had his home-health aides drive him to work, but the agency owners withdrew from his case because their aides were authorized to give only "in-home" care! Marilyn felt she had no right to tell him he should not work. Besides, she said, he would do it anyway! So, she sent him back to work with her blessing with her only condition being to rest if he became tired. As was true before his illness, his family members and employees can be counted on to take David where he needs to go!

In addition to his busy work schedule, David had to find time for his follow-up appointments with his oncologist, Dr. Paramjeet Singh, with Rex-UNC Healthcare. As Diane related in a Facebook post, after his initial hormone injection, her father's PSA level had dropped to 468. On David's next visit, in late September, Dr. Singh excitedly told him that his PSA was at 3.14 (not 314)! Diane added that, during the visit, Dr. Singh kept asking David if he could give him a hug. When David thanked him for his help, Dr. Singh pointed to the sky and gave the credit to God. During the same visit, David had to get an infusion, which took 30 minutes. It is impossible for him to sit still for long without doing something, and he was soon making the rounds of the staff and his fellow patients asking them for their names and where they attend church!

Nowadays, David is filled with gratitude in his heart for how God took a poor country boy like himself from Randolph County, NC, and blessed him and his children in Cary. He is also taking a closer look at how he has impacted people for Christ in recent years. In fact, he believes God has given him more time to live so he can "get his act together." He noted that he had become distracted with a lot of activities which were meant to help others but that he was falling behind on his duty to lead people to Christ. "I've got people working with me on that," he said.

David is not one to sulk or stay down, and, after determining he had fallen short in leading people to Christ, he recently decided to approach a maintenance contractor who had worked with him for 12 years, but with whom he had never spoken about God. "We have people all around us we're not sharing the Gospel of Christ with," David said. David recently decided to broach the subject of eternal salvation with the contractor. When he did, he learned that the man had trouble reading, so David took the time to read and explain the Plan of Salvation to him. Afterward, the man accepted Jesus as his Savior. David gave him a Gideon New Testament, with the manager Sue Lee's signature on the inside back cover as a witness to the contractor's commitment to follow Christ.

Asked what message he would like to leave to his family and friends before the end of his earthly life, David quoted Proverbs 11:30 from the King James Version, "The fruit of the righteous is a tree of life and he that winneth souls is wise."

The Martin grandchildren and spouses or significant others and great-grandchildren. (From left to right) John, Allie, Magnolia and Savannah; Matt; William, Juliana and Emma; Kristen, Nathan and Kinsey; Scott and Katie; Martin, Cassidy and Mason; Patrick: Addison; Parker; Celeste and Brantley; Landon; Alexandra and Justin; Kendell and Rachel; Skyler; Dalton; Cameron and Breanna; Camden; and Abby.

PLAN OF SALVATION

No book about David J. Martin, Sr. would be complete without presenting its readers the Plan of Salvation and giving them the opportunity to respond to it. Below is the Plan of Salvation he shared with anyone willing to listen and that is found in every Gideon Bible he offered to his hearers.

God Loves You

For God so loved the world, that he gave his only begotten Son, that whoever believeth in him should not perish, but have everlasting life. — John 3:16 KJV

But God commandeth his love toward us, in that, while we were still sinners, Christ died for us. — Romans 5:8 KJV

All Are Sinners

For all have sinned and fallen short of the glory of God.—Romans 3:23 KJV

As it is written, there is no one righteous, no not one. — Romans 3:10 KJV

God's Remedy for Sin

For the wages of sin is death; but the gift of God is eternal life through Jesus Christ our Lord. — Romans 6:23 KJV

But as many as received him, to them he gave the power to become the sons of God, even to him that believe on his name. — John 1:12 KJV

For I delivered unto you first of all that which I received, how that Christ died for our sins according to the scriptures; And that he was buried and that he rose again the third day according to the scriptures. —1 Corinthians 15:3-4 KJV

All May be Saved Now

Behold, I stand at the door and knock: if any man hears my voice and opens the door, I will come in to him—Revelation: 3:20 KJV

For whosoever shall call upon the name of the Lord shall be saved. — Romans 10:13 KJV

My Decision to Receive Christ as My Saviour.

Confessing to God that I am a sinner, and believing that the Lord Jesus Christ died for my sins on the cross and was raised for my justification, I do now receive and confess Him as my personal Saviour.

Name:_____

Witness: _____

Date: _____

Assurance as a Believer

That if thou shalt confess with thy mouth the Lord Jesus, and shalt believe in thine heart that God hath raised him from the dead, thou shalt be saved. *Romans 10:9 KJV*

Verily, verily, I say unto you. He that heareth my word and believeth on him who sent me hath everlasting life, and shall not come into condemnation but is passed from death unto life. *John 5:24 KJV*

These things have I written unto you that believe on the name of the Son of God; that ye may know that ye have eternal life, and that ye may believe on the name of the Son of God. — *1 John 5:13 KJV*

Here is a prayer you can say to receive Christ:

"Father, I confess that I am a sinner. I believe that Jesus Christ died for my sins on the cross and was raised for my justification. I do now receive and confess Him as my personal Savior."

Assorted Photos

Chapter 1

Tom Perry, David's maternal grandfather.

Chapter 5

David on a workday while in the Coast Guard.

Anniversary Cake. David Martin, Sr., John Goss, Martin Properties Security and Customer Relations Associate, stand by as Bonnie Campbell, owner of Country Sonshine and South Hills Merchants Association President, and Sue Lee, Martin Properties Receptionist and Office Assistant, cut pieces of the South Hills 30th anniversary cake.

David. Sr., and Mrs. Martin have been blessed to live long enough to see the births of their great-grandchildren. Pictured, on Easter of 2018, are nine of their 13 great-grandchildren. From (L to R) they are: Savanah, Mason, Kinsey, Emma, Brantley, Magnolia, Carli Ann, Henry and his mother Katie; and Della and her mother Cassidy. Not pictured are Kinleigh, Colden, Augie and Ryleigh.

David, Sr. and Marilyn with 19 of their 21 Grandchildren. (Top Row): David, Sr., John, Matt, Marilyn; (Second row) William, Kristen, Scott; (Third row) Martin, Patrick, Addison; (Fourth row) Julia, Parker, Landon; (fifth row) Alexandra, Jill, Kendell; (Bottom Row) Jonni, Sami, Skyler, Dalton, and Cameron.

Miscellaneous

Camden and Abby, the Martins' youngest two grandchildren in 2012.